Praise for

NeuroCoaching

"Leadership is relationship. Without followers, there are no leaders. But just because someone reports to you does not mean they are following you. (They may be spitting in your coffee as they bring it to you.) Docherty and Bloomfield have taken this simple and complex observation to new heights in this engaging and well-grounded-in-research book. As if they have been studying at the Hogwarts of Coaching, they blend the magical potions of shared vision, emotional intelligence, and situational conversations into an explosive and exciting, developmental climate that can bring organizations to new levels of innovation and performance."

—**Richard Boyatzis, PhD**, Distinguished University Professor, Case Western Reserve University, Coauthor of the International Best Seller *Primal Leadership* and *The Science of Change*

"*NeuroCoaching* brings together the neuroscience and social science to give us a new lens to think about leadership. This book is the intersection of executive experience, scholarly models, and practical strategy, demonstrating how building authentic relationships and effective coaching are anything but soft skills. If you want to be a better coach and a more impactful leader, this should be on your reading list."

—**Megan Gerhardt, PhD**, Author of *Gentelligence*, Speaker & Leadership Professor

"NeuroCoaching has transformed our leadership team, empowering us to navigate situational conversations with precision and empathy. By fostering a shared vision and aligned mission, we've cultivated a coaching climate that drives meaningful communication, strengthens collaboration, and accelerates business growth."

—**Rob Truckenmiller**, CEO, PharmaCord

"This book offers a fresh, powerful approach to coaching—blended real-world experience and academic insights to fuel action with trust and purpose. It reminds us that coaching is not about perfection, but progress. A must-read for those looking to make a real impact."

—**David Walters,** Director, MedSurg National Accounts
Boston Scientific

"For all the books there are on coaching, very few endeavor, let alone succeed, in breaking new ground. Even fewer richly detail a road map and define a methodology steeped in science that guides one to achieving predictable success and long-lasting impact.

"Mixed together with the all-in spirit of Docherty and Bloomfield and expressed through their written words coming from a place of genuine care, commitment to cause, and deep authenticity comes *NeuroCoaching*, a must-read for anyone committed to coaching and leading others in a manner that aligns, inspires, engages, elevates, and transforms.

"For those who read *NeuroCoaching*, your best is yet to come."

—**Craig Lucas,** Founder and CEO
Authenica

"*NeuroCoaching* has transformed how our team leads and communicates. Grounded in science and built for impact, it equips leaders to navigate situational coaching conversations, align around a shared vision and mission and foster a strong coaching culture. It's more than training—it's a game-changer for leadership."

—**Tony Esposito,** Life Sciences Executive

"Dr. Docherty and Bloomfield have an incredible talent for communication. This book distills decades of psychological research and data into memorable takeaways and practical strategies. Working daily with executive leaders, I can honestly say that there are very few dilemmas that can't be resolved with the techniques in this book. *NeuroCoaching* pushes coaches and leaders to critically analyze all aspects of their performance so they can work at the cutting-edge and harness the full potential in themselves and their teams."

—**Dr. Iona Naismith,** Clinical Psychologist and Leadership Coach

"*NeuroCoaching* is a masterclass in what matters most—communication. With clarity, compassion, and cutting-edge science, Docherty and Bloomfield offer a practical road map for leaders to transform everyday conversations that define culture, drive performance, and create impactful connection. Grounded in emotional intelligence and neuroscience, this book gives every leader the tools to connect more deeply, lead more intentionally, and coach more effectively. This is the new gold standard for modern leadership."

—**ROBIN EVERHART,** Chief People Officer

"I had the good fortune of working alongside Dan Docherty while scaling a business, and I saw firsthand how he brings the *NeuroCoaching* principles to life. His ability to lean into the tough conversations—the ones that truly shape culture—is unlike anything I've seen. The ideas of shared vision, aligned mission, and situational coaching aren't just concepts in this book; they're real tools we used to lead through both the highs and lows. *NeuroCoaching* is grounded, practical, and it works when it matters most."

—**MATT GARRETSON,** Entrepreneur, Extreme Adventurer, and Author

"As John Wooden's grandson-in-law and author of *Wooden's Wisdom*, I've spent years studying what made Coach Wooden the ultimate situational communicator. This was a key to his success. Coach always knew the right way, time, and tone for every player. Dan Docherty and Jeff Bloomfield's *NeuroCoaching* captures that same art with practical, science-backed insight. Their ability to break down the details of communication strategies for different personalities and pivotal moments is spot on. What Coach Wooden did intuitively, Dan and Jeff explain with clarity and purpose, making this book a valuable resource for leaders, coaches, and parents alike. *NeuroCoaching* is a great read and usable guide to master the critical but subtle craft of great communication. You will be able to use these methods and immediately improve your coaching effectiveness in a significant way."

—**CRAIG IMPELMAN,** Wooden Historian and Author of
Wooden's Wisdom

NEURO
COACHING

Mastering Situational Coaching Conversations
The Neuroscience Behind High-Performing Leaders

DAN DOCHERTY, PHD
JEFF BLOOMFIELD

NeuroCoaching: Mastering Situational Coaching Conversations
The Neuroscience Behind High-Performing Leaders

Copyright © 2025 Dan Docherty, PhD & Jeff Bloomfield. All rights reserved.

No part of this book may be reproduced, stored, or transmitted by any means—whether auditory, graphic, mechanical, or electronic—without written permission of both publisher and author, except in the case of brief excerpts used in critical articles and reviews. Unauthorized reproduction of any part of this work is illegal and is punishable by law.

NeuroCoaching is a trademark of Braintrust, LLC.

For information about this title or to order other books and/or electronic media, contact the publisher:
Published by Braintrust
www.braintrustgrowth.com

ISBN: 978-1-7337870-8-6 (Hardback)
978-1-7337870-9-3 (Paperback)

Printed in the United States

Publishing and Design Services: MelindaMartin.me
Editor: Beth Lottig

CONTENTS

1	**NEUROCOACHING DEFINED**	1
	Top NeuroCoaching Takeaways	10
2	**THE ENGAGEMENT DILEMMA**	11
	Top NeuroCoaching Takeaways	20
3	**THE NEUROSCIENCE OF COACHING: PART 1**	21
	Top NeuroCoaching Takeaways	31
4	**THE NEUROSCIENCE OF COACHING: PART 2**	33
	The "Hand Model" of the Brain's Structure	34
	The Limbic System	37
	The Prefrontal Cortex	40
	Top NeuroCoaching Takeaways	46
5	**NEUROVISIONING**	49
	The Power of a Shared Vision	51
	The Leader's Brain on Vision	54
	Communicating Vision	54
	Inspiring Others	55
	Vision-Driven Decision-Making	55
	Cultivating a Visionary Culture	56
	Neuroplasticity and Adaptation	57
	Top NeuroCoaching Takeaways	59

6　SHARED VISION　　61

NeuroCoaching Playbook: A Case Study in Leadership Transformation　　65
　The Call That Changed Everything　　65
　The NeuroCoaching Playbook: Pillars of Transformation　　65
　The Breakthrough Training That Redefined Leadership　　67
　The Lasting Impact: The Numbers Speak for Themselves　　67

Shared Vision: The Foundation of Coaching Success　　68

The Importance of a Shared Vision and Shared Values　　72

Reflecting Vision and Values through Shared Stories　　73
　Shared Vision - Organizational Level　　75
　Practical Coaching Tips　　78
　Shared Vision – Leader/Coach Level　　79
　A Moment from the Field　　82
　Practical Coaching Tips　　83
　Shared Vision – Employee Level　　84
　Practical Coaching Tips　　85

Top NeuroCoaching Takeaways　　88

7　ALIGNED MISSION　　89

Strategy with Execution: Approach to Strategic Alignment　　90
　Practical Coaching Tips　　96

Standards with Accountability: The Glue That Binds Teams　　97
　Establishing and Upholding Shared Standards　　99
　Practical Coaching Tips　　100

Strengths with Skills: Unlocking Your Talents　　101
　My Strengths Journey:
　Awareness, Activation, and Application　　102
　Strengths in Action: Building High-Performing Teams　　103
　Practical Coaching Tips　　104
　Strengths: A Catalyst for Performance and Purpose　　105

Top NeuroCoaching Takeaways　　107

8	**SITUATIONAL CONVERSATIONS**	**109**
	The Journey of Transformation: A NeuroCoaching Perspective	114
	Situational Conversations: Coaching through the Crossroads	116
	Transformation: When Goals Evolve	117
	The NeuroCoaching Takeaway	117
	Top NeuroCoaching Takeaways	123
9	**CREATING A FLOURISHING COACHING CLIMATE**	**125**
	How to Create a Thriving Coaching Climate	127
	Let's Talk Amplifiers and Dampeners	130
	Top NeuroCoaching Takeaways	136
10	**COACHING CLIMATE AMPLIFIERS:** **LEADERSHIP STYLES & EMOTIONAL INTELLIGENCE**	**137**
	Adaptability in Leadership	140
	Resonant and Dissonant Leadership Styles	142
	Coaching Tip to Activate	144
	Exercise to Activate	145
	Emotional Intelligence	146
	Coaching Tip to Activate	150
	Exercise to Activate	150
	Top NeuroCoaching Takeaways	153
11	**COACHING CLIMATE AMPLIFIERS:** **NEUROQUESTIONING & ACTIVE LISTENING**	**155**
	The Neuroscience of Asking Impactful Questions	156
	Open-Ended versus Closed-Ended Questions	160
	The Power of Active Listening	166
	The Barriers to Effective Listening	167
	Action Steps to Enhance Active Listening	167
	Top NeuroCoaching Takeaways	170

12 COACHING CLIMATE AMPLIFIER: TEAM-BASED PSYCHOLOGICAL SAFETY — 173

- The Power of Psychological Safety — 176
- Coaching Tip to Activate — 178
- Exercise to Activate — 180
- Top NeuroCoaching Takeaways — 182

13 COACHING CLIMATE AMPLIFIER: ORGANIZATIONAL AWARENESS (POWER/POLITICS/INFLUENCE) — 183

- The Nature of Power and Influence — 185
- Stories from the Frontlines — 186
  - Building a Broad Network — 187
  - Understanding the Informal Structure — 187
  - Staying Authentic — 188
  - Advocating for Transparency — 188
  - Building Alliances — 191
  - Managing Conflicts — 190
  - Communicating Effectively — 190
  - Leveraging Neuroscience Principles: Emotional Intelligence (EI) — 191
  - Building Trust — 192
  - Activating the Right Brain Networks — 193
- Practical Strategies for Leaders — 193
  - Conducting Power Audits — 194
  - Developing Political Savvy — 194
  - Enhancing Communication Skills — 195
- Top NeuroCoaching Takeaways — 196

14 COACHING CLIMATE AMPLIFIERS: THE IMPACT OF VR/AR AND AI ON COACHING — 199

- Leadership Development Gets Real (Virtually) — 200
  - AI: Your Personal Performance Coach — 200
  - Emotional Intelligence: Practice Makes Perfect — 201
  - Revolutionizing Sales Training — 201

The Neuroscience behind It All	203
Emotions and Learning: A Powerful Combo	203
Repetition: The Key to Mastery	204
The Democratization of Coaching	204
Creating Safe Environments for Learning	204
Challenges and Potential Drawbacks	205
The Human Touch	205
Privacy and Ethical Concerns	205
The Digital Divide	205
The Future of Coaching: A Brave New World	206
Wrapping It Up	207
Top NeuroCoaching Takeaways	208

15   CASE STUDY & COACHING THOUGHTS   209

Case Study: Coaching for Career Growth in Life Sciences	210
The NeuroCoaching® Leadership Development Approach	211
Key Measurement Goals	211
Client Testimonial	211
Coaching Scenario: Preparing for a Promotion Opportunity	212
Coaching Situation	212
Situational Conversation Road Map (The Stoplight Approach)	212
Key Takeaways for NeuroCoaching Learners	215
Situational Coaching Conversations – Your Turn	216
Scenario Play: Running the Coaching Playbook on Five Situations	216
Step 1: Select a Coaching Scenario	216
The 6P's Framework for Situational Coaching Conversations	217
Your Challenge: Run This Playbook on Five Coaching Scenarios	219
Final Thought: Breaking through the Stoplights	220
Coaching Thoughts	220

	A Leadership Perspective: Coach Nick Saban	223
	Our Responsibility as Leaders	224
	Top NeuroCoaching Takeaways	226

16   PUTTING IT ALL TOGETHER: CREATING COACHING COMMUNICATION HABITS   227

	Creating Communication Habits: The Conscious Competence Model	229
	Scenario 1: The 1:1 Development Conversation	232
	Scenario 2: The Pop-Up Conversation	232
	Scenario 3: The Observational Skill Follow-Up	233
	Scenario 4: The Team Coaching Session	233
	Scenario 5: The Performance Review	234
	Top NeuroCoaching Takeaways	236

17   HOW TO HAVE AN IMPACT AT THE HIGHEST LEVEL   237

ACKNOWLEDGMENTS	**243**
BIBLIOGRAPHY	**245**
ENDNOTES	**256**
ABOUT THE AUTHORS	**265**

CHAPTER 1

NEUROCOACHING DEFINED

The greatest coaches aren't just game changers; they are life changers.
—TONY DUNGY

THE FLUORESCENT LIGHTS in the conference room flickered slightly, casting an unforgiving glow over the tense figures seated at the table. At the time, I was a seasoned manager at a high-profile biotech firm. I tapped my pen against the table, a rhythm to my unconscious anxiety. Across the table, Chris, a key member of my team, seemed to be clenching his fists, bracing for the conversation we were about to have. It had been a challenging quarter. The market was evolving at breakneck speed, and the team was under immense pressure to innovate and deliver. I was feeling the weight of expectations from the senior executives above me and had been pushing the team harder than ever. Chris, once a star performer, had been struggling to keep up.

I could feel my heart rate increasing as I prepared to have this difficult conversation. I thought back to my own experiences early in my career when I had been on the receiving end of "constructive" feedback from managers who didn't take the time to understand my perspective. I remembered the sinking feeling in my gut, the sense of failure and inadequacy that made it hard to stay motivated. I didn't want to make Chris feel that way, but I also knew we couldn't afford any slippage in performance right now. This was a make-or-break moment for the team.

The air was thick with unspoken tension as I began, my voice betraying a hint of frustration. "Chris, your performance these past few months has not been up to the usual standards. We're at a critical juncture, and we need everyone at their best. I need to see significant improvement, or we'll have to consider other options." As the words hung in the air, I studied Chris's face, seeing the barely concealed look of hurt and disappointment wash over his features.

Chris took a deep breath, struggling to keep his emotions in check. "I've been giving it my all. The expectations keep changing, and it's been tough to know where I stand. I need more support, not just more pressure." His voice cracked slightly on the last word, revealing the depth of his discouragement.

My brow furrowed as my mind raced to make sense of Chris's reaction. I had expected defensiveness, but this seemed like something more.

Let's take a brief time-out from our story. Has there been a time when you were in Chris's shoes, frustrated and unsupported by your manager during a high-pressure situation? Or perhaps you've been in my position, struggling to have a difficult performance conversation in a productive way? Take a moment to reflect on how you felt in that moment and how you responded.

Let's continue on with our story . . .

My defenses were up, and feeling as though he clearly wasn't "getting it," I barged ahead blindly. "Look, Chris, the numbers don't lie. Your productivity has taken a nosedive lately, and I really can't understand why. I need you to get it together quickly, or we're going to have to rethink your role on this team."

Chris recoiled as if he'd been physically struck. "You have no idea how hard I've been working! I put in countless hours; I ask for help and get nowhere. This is unfair."

"Unfair?" My voice took an almost exasperated edge. "What's unfair is me getting peppered by my boss every day about why things haven't improved. What's unfair is me trying to pick up your slack so others don't notice you're falling further behind. What's unfair is having a key team member not putting in the work when we're all burning the midnight oil. I don't have time to coddle underperformers."

The flames of resentment burned hot in Chris's eyes as the defensive distance between us stretched into a chasm. As he stormed out, I knew instantly that I had handled that in the worst possible way. But my pride wouldn't let me acknowledge it—not yet, anyway.

Depending on the culture you exist in and the "coaching climate" that exists within that culture, you may think that this conversation was absurd and would never take place on your team, or you might have actually felt a tinge of stress just reading it because it hit all too close to home. It's important to understand that these types of conversations are usually a result of weeks and months of ongoing unproductive interactions, not just an isolated moment. Reflecting on my journey as a manager, this story marks yet another challenging dialogue in a long line of them. However, when I juxtapose my years of leadership in corporate America with nearly two decades spent researching the neuroscience of high-performance communication, the realization hits hard: I can scarcely grasp the magnitude of how off the mark I was in many of my coaching conversations. This acknowledgment isn't just a recount of past errors but a vulnerable admission of my ongoing evolution and the emotional investment it demands, both from myself and those who have been on the receiving end of a management style that's intuitively more pacesetting and commanding than it is empathic and compassionate.

This story is unfortunately not unique to just my experience. It's a scene that plays out in various forms across countless organizations. And it underscores a critical, often overlooked truth: The way we communicate, especially under stress, can have profound implications on performance, engagement, and retention. According to Gallup, nearly 70 percent of employees are either disengaged (quietly quitting) or actively disengaged (loudly quitting) at work.[1] This disengagement is a silent killer of productivity and morale, a barrier to innovation and growth. But perhaps even more telling is that 50 percent of employees who leave their companies cite their manager as the number one reason for their departure.[2] This clearly indicates that there is a problem we must all face. These statistics are not just numbers; they are a stark reminder of the cost of missed connections and miscommunication between managers and their teams.

Let's see what *could* have happened in an alternative universe where I went back in time and mentored myself with all the knowledge you will receive by the end of this book.

Chris took a deep breath, struggling to keep his emotions in check. "I've been giving it my all. The expectations keep changing, and it's been tough to know where I stand. I need more support, not just more pressure." His voice cracked slightly on the last word, revealing the depth of his discouragement.

A tiny voice in the back of my mind whispered that I might be missing something important here.

Drawing on my training in emotional intelligence as part of the NeuroCoaching® program, I made an effort to pause and really listen to what Chris was saying beneath the surface. I heard the plea for clarity and coaching and the need for a new plan and better path to help him get back on track. And I realized that, in my single-minded focus on results, I had failed to provide the supportive guidance he needed.

The conversation could have easily spiraled from there, with both of us digging in our heels and the situation devolving into a bitter clash of egos.

But at that pivotal moment, my training kicked in. I took a deep breath and adjusted my approach.

"Chris, you're absolutely right. As I consider your perspective, I suppose I haven't been giving you the kind of support and direction you need to succeed in this rapidly changing environment. That's on me, and I'm committed to doing better." I leaned forward, making eye contact. "Why don't you walk me through what you're struggling with right now? I'm here to listen and to help get you the resources you need."

As Chris began to open up, I made a conscious effort to resist the urge to jump in with solutions right away. Instead, I focused on asking empathic questions, trying to further understand his perspective and the root causes of his challenges. It wasn't easy—my natural instinct was to take charge, give him the answers, and start delegating tasks. But I could sense Chris's defenses lowering as he realized I was genuinely interested in seeing things from his point of view.

What followed was a frank but collaborative discussion where Chris felt safe to express his concerns, and I was able to provide targeted guidance and support. We identified specific areas where additional training or process improvements could help streamline Chris's workflow. I also committed to weekly one-on-one coaching sessions to ensure he had a consistent forum to get unstuck and realign on priorities. We landed on a new plan, and we agreed on how we would measure progress and recognize success.

As the meeting wrapped up, I could sense the shift in the atmosphere, what we will refer to in this book as the coaching climate. The tension had dissipated, replaced by a shared sense of purpose and mutual understanding and a recommitment to shared standards that were necessary for Chris, me as his manager, and the company to all succeed. Chris seemed reenergized, his body language more confident and open. And I felt a profound sense of relief that I had navigated that critical conversation in a way that brought my team member closer rather than pushing him away.

We'll talk later about how much time we, as coaches, spend looking in the rearview mirror versus the windshield. But as I take a long, hard look in my own rearview, I see now the pivotal turn the situation could have taken had I approached it differently. At the time, my emotional awareness and control were not what they should have been. Caught up in my frustrations and singularly focused on outcomes, I was on the brink of pushing a valuable team member away—a mistake we could hardly afford. The alternative path—had I had the right training and support—involved genuinely attempting to understand Chris's challenges from his perspective, all while guiding us toward the necessary improvements. This approach would not only have preserved our relationship but also fostered a collaborative environment conducive to mutual growth and success.

Let me be crystal clear on one glaring point: This isn't about being overly empathetic with no real accountability for results... just the opposite. It's about using the tools you'll learn in this book to drive *more* accountability and *better,* more sustainable results by adjusting the way in which you handle these situations. Not by using instinct or intuition. Not by drastically altering your personality or leadership style but by applying a proven and clear set of communication principles rooted in decades of research.

In hindsight, recognizing and adjusting my approach could have been the key to turning a potential conflict into a powerful moment of connection. With every conversation we have as leader/coaches, we have an opportunity to improve trust without compromising truth. It's all in the way we choose to communicate.

As you read through these two very different ways I handled the scenario with Chris, what thoughts or feelings came up for you? Could you relate to the resentment and defensiveness in the first example? Or perhaps you recognized some of your own communication blind spots or knee-jerk reactions in conversations you've had with team members?

In the second scenario, where I afforded myself a rearview fictitious "mulligan" (a golf term indicating a second chance), I took a radically different approach—one rooted in the principles of neuroscience and emotional intelligence. This event served as a powerful reminder of the importance of intentional communication as a leader, an approach rooted in science rather than gut instinct. It highlighted how the way we communicate, especially in high-stakes, high-stress situations, can have far-reaching ripple effects on performance, engagement, and retention.

Now, imagine a world where leaders and managers wield that kind of superpower—a profound understanding of the human brain that transforms their approach to coaching, driving unprecedented engagement and performance across their teams. Welcome to the world of NeuroCoaching, a realm where science and leadership converge to create a revolutionary approach to empowerment and success.

For decades, the fields of neuroscience and behavioral psychology have been unraveling the mysteries of the human mind, providing insights that have the potential to redefine the art of leadership. Yet, despite this wealth of knowledge, a gap has persisted—a disconnect between what science knows and what leadership does—until now.

As we embark on this journey, remember: The goal is not just to lead but to inspire, not just to manage but to empower. We are in pursuit of a place where intentionality and understanding pave the way for unparalleled performance and engagement. The heart of effective leadership lies not only in intuition but intentionality. It's not about leading based on a hunch but about understanding the why behind the what. It's about leveraging the incredible power of the brain to foster environments where communication flourishes, relationships deepen, and performance soars.

At the core of NeuroCoaching is a groundbreaking approach to forming a foundational *shared vision* followed by a situational coaching framework born from decades of research and the collective wisdom of leading institutions and thought leaders. This isn't just another leadership development program, and it's not another run-of-the-mill acronym-based coaching model; it's a transformational journey that begins with the alignment of that *shared vision*: organizational, leader, and employee, the triad that forms the foundation upon which productive and meaningful *coaching conversations* are built, ultimately guided by a *six-step situational conversation framework* designed to unlock potential like never before.

By weaving the principles of NeuroCoaching into the stories you will encounter in this book, we not only make the science more accessible—we make it unforgettable. In doing so, we empower leaders to shift from intuitive to intentional leadership, from guessing games to a deep, evidence-based understanding of what truly drives human behavior and performance.

Our intent with this work, while co-authored, is to present a cohesive perspective from a single, unified voice. You may notice stories that identify the speaker in some way, but we've done our best to stay out of the way so the message, purpose, and impact of NeuroCoaching can shine through. As you turn these pages, you'll hopefully find yourself on a journey of discovery and growth. You'll see the world of leadership through a new lens, one that illuminates the path to truly effective communication and coaching. This is not about giving you an entirely new coaching toolbox; it's about equipping you with newer, modern tools that will allow you to be more effective with the coaching toolbox you already have, assuming you believe your job is to drive performance by developing people. It's about becoming the kind of leader who knows how to unlock the full potential of their team, not by chance, but by design.

Before we begin in full, I would ask you to do a bit of self-reflection. In my experience, depending on where you are in your career and what exposure to great coaching you may have received to this point, there could be a few barriers preventing you from getting the most from the information contained in this book. For some, we resist change out of fear. For others, we resist out of pride. To be transparent, I've done both, especially early in my career. If fear or pride are in the driver's seat, then humility and empathy are likely in the backseat or, even worse, the trunk! I can tell you from experience that due to my lack of training, lack of mentorship, and inherent personality flaws—where I needed to be seen as having the answers—my leadership positions had their ups and downs. Whether you're a first-year manager or a seasoned executive, I promise you that what you'll discover in this book and through our research and practice isn't just information revealed through a couple of guys' opinions. It will also likely contain some information you may already know but might see through a different lens. More than likely, much of what you will find here will be new and certainly novel in the way we present the *application* of this information in your day-to-day communication approach as a coach.

Allow me to share a guiding principle that shapes my daily life, one which I believe will set the stage for you to engage with the insights of this book most effectively: the understanding that there's always something new to learn and there's always an approach to being a better leader and coach that you may not have considered. If you continue turning the pages of this book with that mindset, you will thrive with the new knowledge and tools you will learn here. On the other hand, if you have already arrived at your "world-class level" desired coaching destination, you need not go any further. But I'd be willing to bet that's not who you are, or you wouldn't have picked this book up to begin with.

With that in mind, are you ready to embark on this transformative journey? Are you prepared to uncover the secrets of the brain that will set you and your team on a path to unparalleled success? Let's dive in. The adventure of NeuroCoaching awaits.

Top NeuroCoaching Takeaways

1. **Communication under stress can make or break a team.**

   The way managers communicate during high-pressure situations has profound effects on employee engagement, performance, and retention. A lack of communication in leadership conversations can lead to disengagement, resentment, and even turnover.

2. **Emotional intelligence is crucial in leadership conversations.**

   The alternative scenario with Chris demonstrates that pausing to listen, showing empathy, and understanding an employee's perspective can lead to better outcomes.

3. **Instinct-driven leadership is ineffective compared to science-backed coaching.**

   Leaders often rely on gut feelings when handling difficult conversations, but neuroscience and behavioral psychology offer a more effective, evidence-based approach. NeuroCoaching equips managers with practical tools to drive sustainable performance improvements.

CHAPTER 2

THE ENGAGEMENT DILEMMA

If the corporate world creates more skilled team leaders, companies will produce better results, and employees will have more fun doing it.
—Tom Brady

SIMILARLY TO JEFF, I myself struggled at times when leading effectively within the four walls of my life sciences company when I became a general manager. I saw firsthand how stress quietly crept in and unraveled both my own performance and my team's. The weight of expectations was relentless, and the decline—though subtle at first—was undeniable.

Step out of my shoes for a moment and imagine your own office. When you walk in every morning, do you notice seven or so people quietly quitting? What about loudly quitting?

The shift can start slowly—your one employee, who would arrive early, now comes in later and later. Another, who was once an active participant in meetings, hardly ever speaks up now. After a while, you might realize that your entire team is suffering from an *engagement dilemma*.[1]

My company was undergoing a huge change at the time, and I was swept up in needing higher outputs from the employees. Pressure could be felt across all our offices, and the walls of the company—once filled with energy and purpose—felt like they were closing in. As a result, my coaching skills were suffering. One-on-one conversations became shallow, and my "open door policy" was a relic of the past. I was too busy to engage, and therefore, my team's growth and development suffered. And what's worse is that this probably sounds familiar to you.

It's time we be real with ourselves as leaders.

The concept of an engagement dilemma isn't new, but it certainly has been amplified as we have more employees than ever before working virtually, implementing flex scheduling, and reflecting on their future within our organizations.

> *The Great Reflection led to the Great Resignation that is NOW the Great Fight for Talent.*[2]

Let's look introspectively for a moment. Here are a few questions for you to reflect on as we dig deeper into NeuroCoaching.

In any given situational coaching conversation, can you answer these questions:

1. Do you have a shared vision for where your team member desires to go?

2. Do your conversations have a clearly stated purpose?

3. Do you consider the other person's perspective before the conversation?

4. Do you have a clear, agreed-upon, co-developed action plan?

5. Can your team member identify if they are on or off the desired path?

6. Does your team member proactively come to you to measure progress?

7. Are problems identified in advance?

8. Have you clearly defined what performance looks like to achieve the goals for your team member?

These questions set the foundation for NeuroCoaching. We have found that when these questions aren't answered consistently, then we're adding more fuel to the engagement crisis. The dilemma is that leaders want high employee engagement, yet, year after year, we and our team members aren't becoming more engaged.

As we unpack this chapter, you're going to see that the engagement crisis is real, and it's impacted by the conversations we, as leaders, have every day with the people we're entrusted to lead and influence.

I'll never forget that one December day when we mapped out the plan to launch NeuroCoaching. Over the past three-plus years, we've been fortunate to have some of the world's top companies and leaders place their trust in this approach. Intentional coaching—rooted in shared vision, aligned mission, and situational conversations—created a climate that not only transformed performance but also changed lives within companies.

During my PhD journey, I learned that effective research begins with identifying a problem of practice. This problem informs the research question, which then guides the development of a sustainable system in the chosen field. Our goal is to provide you with a sustainable system for impactful conversations, whether during one-on-ones or in the boardroom.

However, when I first started my PhD degree at Case Western, I didn't fully understand why our management program was called "Designing a Sustainable System"—in fact, I questioned one of my professors about the title. He told me that the title wouldn't matter to anyone outside of the program, so just call it a management degree. In the moment, I accepted this. But after a couple of years studying systems of thinking, decision-making, and complexity theory, I realized that the title was actually brilliant. If we reset our thinking about leadership coaching as a system, we can then break down the parts (which we will do), understand the problem of practice, and then rebuild it from a first principles reasoning approach.

> ***First principles reasoning*** *is a problem-solving approach that breaks down complex ideas into their most basic, fundamental truths and then builds up solutions from there, rather than relying on assumptions or past experiences.*

No matter what you think about polarizing leaders like Elon Musk, he and many others use this reasoning approach when leading new endeavors. For example, instead of assuming batteries are expensive because they always have been, Elon analyzed their raw materials, calculated their actual costs, and instead found ways to cheaply manufacture them. This method has allowed him to be innovative in industries like space travel, electric vehicles, AI, and now even government waste.

With this in mind, we'll break down the parts of leadership coaching by first unpacking the problem of practice and engagement crisis. We're getting to the root and growing from there.

In today's current climate, team members are often disengaged, aren't staying as long as they used to, and may even be leaving you. Good people are leaving good jobs and their leaders.[3] Yes, many employees used to state that they would quit due to bad managers (and that is true); however, now they're even leaving good ones.

Many of us have had access to Gallup's work on employee engagement that they've been surveying for decades, and their Q12 is a great tool to gauge current engagement levels. They've measured over 3.3 million workers across 100,000+ teams.[4] Spanning the topics of expectations at work, relationships, recognition, and organizational mission and purpose, the Q12 survey gets to the heart of employee engagement.

When you reflect on the engagement of your own team, how would your employees respond to questions about their professional development, your communication of the company's mission and purpose, or the utilization of their strengths?

Last year, we were working on a project with a major hospital system, and they designed a yearlong learning development program called Engage 2024. We were fortunate to be a part of leading four of the sessions throughout the year with eighty leaders. They evaluated the Q12 and wanted to dig into four aspects of engagement. These sessions were outlined in the following way: *know me, focus me, hear me,* and *challenge me*. As we navigated the program, we broke down each of these topics into their fundamental truths and built them back from there. We didn't look at engagement as a topic but rather as an outcome of building sustainable relationships in a very stressful work environment.

If we want to break down engagement, we can utilize tools like Gallup and define engagement in a way that might shed some light for us all in practice.

I want to give you a practical way to look at engagement as how much **vigor**, **dedication**, and **absorption** your team members bring to their job every day.

Vigor can be defined as how much **energy** your team members bring every day. Do you ever realize that you're spending over 250 days a year and 2,000+ hours with your team members? Let's take this a step further: How dedicated are they, not only to their jobs but to you, the team, and the organization? How absorbed are they in their work?

What about you, though? How much vigor, dedication, and absorption do you bring every day? We, as leader/coaches, help create the environment for the people we serve.

Quickly jot down a list of the people you lead and simply place them in either an "engaged" or "disengaged" category. Then, think about why they might be engaged or disengaged. What's the climate you're creating within these individuals and the team? I'm asking a lot of questions because we, as leaders, have to turn the mirror toward ourselves first in order to realize the impact we're having on those we lead.

Here's what Gallup is reporting in their 2024 State of the Global Workplace report:[5]

1. 31 percent Thriving at Work (engaged)

2. 52 percent Quiet Quitting (not engaged)

3. 17 percent Loud Quitting (actively disengaged)

Remember those seven employees in your office I mentioned earlier who might be quietly or loudly quitting? These stats reinforce that almost 70 percent of the workforce is either not currently engaged or is actively disengaged at work. So even if this is partially accurate, we all still have an epidemic within the workplace just as we are recovering from a pandemic. Gallup's additional insights for the US as a region have the following takeaway points:

1. Highest regional percent of daily stress.

2. Second highest percent who say now is a good time to look for a job.

3. Highest percent of female employees who experience high daily stress.

Take a look at it this way: If engagement levels are low and turnover high, what's the common denominator? Research consistently points to leadership. Gallup's studies suggest that over 50 percent of the time, it's the leader—that's you or me—who's influencing whether people stay or go.[6]

> If engagement levels are low and turnover high, what's the common denominator? Research consistently points to leadership.

The manager-team member relationship is at the heart of this crisis. Poor coaching, ineffective communication, and lack of development opportunities drive disengagement. Leaders and team members have reported on the causes of conflict in their jobs, and the number one reason was inept criticism by a boss.[7] Employee perception of the organizational climate can be traced to the boss, and more than anyone else, they directly determine people's ability to work well.[8]

If that isn't a critical situation, I don't know what is. But here's the good news: We can change that.

When I was struggling to keep my head above water as a general manager, I didn't know what to do. But looking back, that season of struggle became the catalyst that led me to Case Western Reserve University, where I began studying the impact of coaching and development within the leader–team member dynamic. Along the way, I met my co-author, and together we began to dream. We envisioned a new approach to leadership coaching—one grounded in both science and practical experience. If we, as leader/coaches, want to have a high development culture, there are factors within our control.

First, if we serve as a CEO or a senior leader in an organization, we have to be all in. Otherwise, all these programs we're trying to implement won't have an impact. Second, we, as leader coaches, need to move from the mindset of a boss to a coach. Remember Jeff's story from the last chapter? His ego as a boss formed a wall between his employee and himself when he really needed to be a coach. Third, communication matters. Company communication and the consistency of that communication matters.

Fourth, we must hold ourselves accountable, and we can by creating a climate where we focus on development, inspiration, flourishing, giving back, hard work, conversation impact, situational fluency, and performance.

Our team members are hungry for coaching, and we can make a difference every day in every conversation. But we need to increase our skill set and leverage situational moments of impact—but what's a situational moment of impact?

As leaders, we step into a dynamic environment of constant communication each day. Our conversations are shaped by structure—some are carefully planned, while others emerge in the moment. The format of these interactions continues to evolve; for example, we're now several years past the widespread adoption of virtual platforms like Teams and Zoom, and it's time to normalize turning cameras on to create a more connected, human experience. From spontaneous hallway chats to scheduled one-on-ones with direct reports, strategic discussions with peers and managers, and broader team or organizational meetings, the variety is endless. In fact, it's estimated that the average professional engages in over twenty-five to thirty conversations a day,[9] making the ability to navigate these moments with intention not just important but *essential* for effective leadership. See the graphic below.

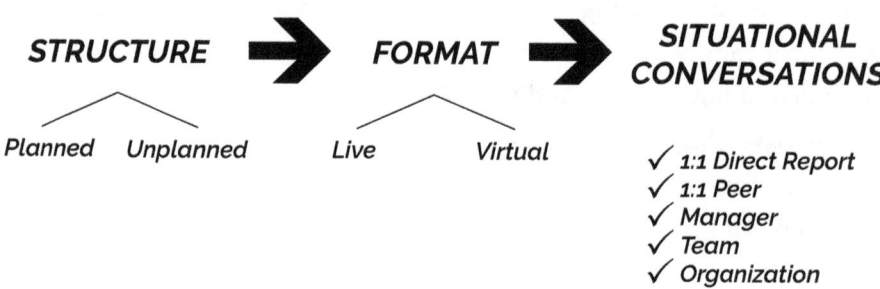

I'd make the argument that there's nothing more important than improving your communication and coaching skills. We need to shift from being bosses to being coaches, focusing on development, communication, and accountability. Every day, every minute, every hour, we stack up these situational moments of impact that can either build up or tear down a relationship. And relationships rarely stay in the status quo. So every day, every conversation, we need to come from a place of trust and truth if we want to lean into driving higher performance.

A way to do this is through PIP, but before you sigh and flip the page, realize that I'm not talking about a "performance improvement plan" but rather a *Purpose, Impact,* and *Performance* plan that can change your own coaching dynamic for the better.

Let's dive in and explore how NeuroCoaching can help you lead with purpose, impact, and performance.

> Every day, in every conversation, we need to come from a place of trust and truth if we want to lean into driving higher performance.

Is this causing a bit of stress? I hope so. But I also hope it inspires you to listen to not only this but our other concepts as we go through this book. There's a gap in how leaders are incorporating knowledge into their daily coaching routines. If this problem was solved, we wouldn't be writing this book, and you wouldn't be reading it. Our desire is to help fill that gap, and the time to change is now.

Top NeuroCoaching Takeaways

1. **Employee engagement is in a crisis.**

    Nearly 70 percent of employees are either quietly or loudly quitting. Research consistently points to leadership as the primary reason, meaning managers must take responsibility for fostering an environment where employees feel motivated, valued, and supported.

2. **The "fight for talent" is reshaping the workforce.**

    Employees today are reevaluating their career paths, so companies that don't invest in leadership development and coaching cultures will continue to struggle with retention.

3. **Communication, accountability, and development are nonnegotiable.**

    Strong leadership requires clear communication, consistent messaging, and a structured development approach. Leaders must be intentional about setting expectations, providing feedback, and fostering a climate where employees understand their roles and contributions. The "purpose, impact, and performance" (PIP) framework offers a much different model for improving coaching conversations and driving better results than the usual "performance improvement plan" style.

CHAPTER 3

THE NEUROSCIENCE OF COACHING: PART 1

Leaders who ignore evidence are either naïve, irresponsible, or both.
—Jeffrey Pfeffer and Robert Sutton

WHEN I BEGAN my journey to better understand the brain and its connection to leadership, I was fortunate to work alongside researchers like Anthony Jack, Richard Boyatzis, and Ellen Van Oosten on my PhD team. Dr. Jack leads a team at the Brain, Mind, and Consciousness Lab at Case Western Reserve University (CWRU) in Cleveland, OH, and Boyatzis and Van Oosten co-lead the Coaching Research Lab at CWRU. Their groundbreaking research, showcased in their award-winning 2018 article "The Neuroscience of Coaching," introduces two crucial brain networks: the analytical network (AN) and the empathic network (EN).[1]

As detailed in *Helping People Change*, these networks each play unique roles. The analytical network (AN) is activated when we need to solve problems, analyze information, make decisions, and focus. It's the network we rely on when we need clear, logical thinking. In contrast, the empathic network (EN) allows us to be open to new ideas, observe trends and patterns, connect with others emotionally, and consider moral concerns—truly understanding others' perspectives instead of just making judgments about what's "right" or "wrong."

Imagine the implications of this for coaching. The AN and EN operate independently, and when one is active, it tends to suppress the other. As coaches and leaders, we need to skillfully cycle between these networks, using *both* to be effective. For example, when our team members focus on analytical tasks, they engage the AN, diving into logical thinking. But when they engage in social tasks, like helping or empathizing with others, the EN activates, opening them up to new ideas, people, and emotions.[2]

Understanding this dynamic is crucial for coaches. With *intentional* effort, we can activate each network to foster growth, learning, and development in those we lead. Additional findings from fMRI (functional magnetic resonance imaging: brain-imaging technique used to measure and map brain activity) studies show that positive, supportive approaches in coaching are significantly more effective than negative, critical approaches. Positive coaching methods activate brain regions that "open up" individuals, encouraging them to explore and make their own choices rather than shutting down in defensiveness.[3]

To see how this applies practically in a business setting, consider a typical performance review. Suppose we, as coaches, enter the review feeling stressed and focus primarily on facts, data, KPIs, and goals. This approach naturally activates our own analytical network, which may unintentionally suppress our capacity for empathy. In response, the team member's brain also shifts into analytical mode, but this often leads to feeling judged and under scrutiny rather than supported. As a result, the empathic network in their brain—the part that helps them stay open to feedback—gets suppressed, leading to increased skepticism and resistance.

THE INCORRECT COMMUNICATION APPROACH
Analytical Overactivation

INFORMATION TYPE	Entry Point of Conversation - Data/Information	More Information, More Evaluation	Skepticism and Judgment	Uncertainty, Risk, and Resistance

ANALYTICAL NETWORK (NEOCORTEX)

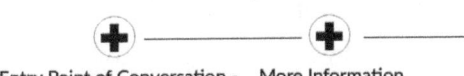
NOREPINEPHRINE (ADRENALINE)

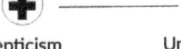
CORTISOL (STRESS)

EMPATHIC NETWORK (LIMBIC/ROOT)

SUPPRESSED/INACTIVE

OXYTOCIN (TRUST)

DOPAMINE (REWARD)

End Result:
Distrust, Rejection, No Commitment

This overly analytical approach is like flooding a conversation with facts and figures without any warmth or connection. While the intent may be to drive results, it often has the opposite effect, building distrust and closing down the person's openness to new ideas. In turn, this stifles growth and diminishes their willingness to change.

Now, let's consider a different scenario. This time, we enter a performance review with the intention of engaging the empathic network (EN), so we start the conversation on a more personal note (please make this authentic; talking about the weather or sports isn't good enough)—perhaps sharing a story or discussing something relatable. As the conversation progresses, we build on this connection, diving deeper into casual and personal topics.

While this approach certainly fosters goodwill and likability, it may not achieve the intended outcome. In this scenario, we've created a strong emotional connection, but we haven't introduced any urgency or clear direction for improvement. As a result, we end up with a connection that feels good emotionally but lacks a commitment to change or specific guidance on performance expectations.

Here, we've over-activated the empathic network, suppressing the analytical network. This is like sharing a warm, engaging story without ever getting to the point. We're creating rapport, but we're not providing the structure or direction needed to drive performance.

In this case, we've veered too far toward empathy without balancing it with the analytical focus that's also necessary for effective coaching.

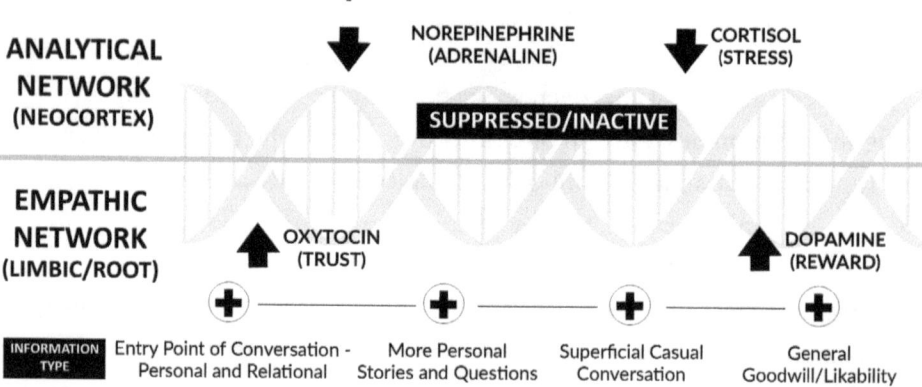

To support the extensive research on this subject, let me introduce a blended approach to coaching. Think of this method as an "emotion coaster." Returning to our performance review example, let's approach the conversation by first engaging the empathic network (EN). This way, our team members feel open to new ideas. We begin with a two-way dialogue, sharing information and discussing insights that allow the analytical network (AN) to step in naturally. This *balanced navigation with situational fluency*—engaging empathy while inviting analysis—helps prevent either network from being overdriven.

We recommend leading with empathy and activating compassion (empathy in action), as this opens the door to connection and trust. As a coach, this approach allows you to activate both networks intentionally and authentically. Of course, there are moments when it's appropriate to activate only the analytical network, focusing on data and goals. Other times, it's better to lean exclusively into the empathic network, creating rapport and understanding. The most effective coaches know when to use each network—and, importantly, how to balance both—to impact conversations from the water cooler to the boardroom.

Think of it like this: Connection and empathy without direction and urgency might make you a well-liked leader, but they won't drive results. On the other hand, direction and urgency without empathy and connection may make you seem callous and demanding, which can increase defensiveness and decrease engagement.

> The most effective coaches know when to use each network—and, importantly, how to balance both—to impact conversations from the water cooler to the boardroom.

The skill lies in learning to guide both networks at the right time, with the right information, and in the right order. As the ever-wise Michael Scott from *The Office* said when asked whether he'd prefer to be loved or feared, "I want people to be afraid of how much they love me." A humorous but fitting reminder that balance—using both networks appropriately—creates true influence.

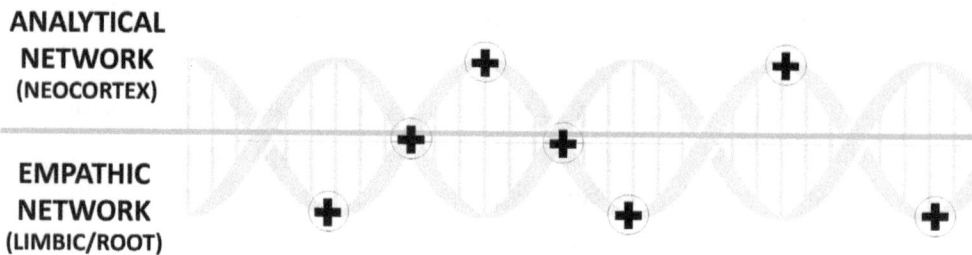

In *Helping People Change*, the authors provide a great equation to put this all together:

PEA (Positive Emotional Attractors) = EN + PNS + positive feelings

NEA (Negative Emotional Attractors) = AN + SNS + negative feelings[4,5]

When we leverage personal connection and show empathy for another person—demonstrating care for what they care about—it often activates their parasympathetic nervous system (PNS), releasing hormones and neurotransmitters like oxytocin. The PNS sets off our body's "renewal processes," which include stimulation of the vagus nerve and secretion of oxytocin, often called the "bonding hormone." Oxytocin's impact can be profound, opening blood vessels, reducing blood pressure and pulse rate, and encouraging deeper, slower breaths. Think of it as the body's "rest and restore" signal, creating a state of calm readiness.[6]

On the other hand, when we lead with a heavy emphasis on credibility—perhaps coming across as all business or overly critical—we risk activating the sympathetic nervous system (SNS), which releases cortisol and other stress-related hormones. As discussed earlier, this stress response speeds up pulse rate and increases blood pressure, causing shallower, quicker breathing as your body gears up to confront a challenge. When this stress cascade occurs, cortisol eventually enters the bloodstream. While cortisol has its benefits—sharpening our focus and acting as a natural anti-inflammatory—it also suppresses the immune system and, when prolonged, can lead to burnout.

Chronic stress puts the body in a constant "ready for battle" mode, leading to cognitive, perceptual, and emotional impairment as the body prioritizes survival over rest and renewal.[7] Here, the research is again about balance and timing: We need both oxytocin and cortisol, but they must be triggered in the right sequence and kept in check. Throughout this book, you will see a mega theme about balance.

Imagine the difference in how you feel after a day or two of vacation compared to a high-pressure work week. That vacation renewal feeling is your PNS at work, restoring your body and mind. Now, picture a pacesetting or commanding style leader who constantly drives their team without balancing stress with empathy—like a car always in high gear. Without knowing how to "shift down" or activate a calming influence, such leadership creates chronic stress that impacts not only physical health but also relationships and overall performance. Over time, a chronic state of stress can wear down even the best performers, affecting their resilience and capacity for growth.

Additional findings in fMRI support the theoretical predictions that the Positive Emotional Attractor (PEA) is associated with visioning and engagement of the PNS and Negative Emotional Attractor (NEA) of the

SNS, which impact motivation.[8] Here, visioning is defined as a "mental process in which images of the desired future (goals, objectives, outcomes) are made intensely real and compelling to act as motivators for the present action."[9]

> Over time, a chronic state of stress can wear down even the best performers, affecting their resilience and capacity for growth.

How exactly does neuroscience support the idea of coaching to facilitate development? Recent findings from a brain-imaging study show that *coaching with compassion*—known as coaching to the Positive Emotional Attractor (PEA)—activates regions of the brain associated with positive emotion and visioning, while suppressing the Negative Emotional Attractor (NEA). Compassionate coaching activates areas associated with big-picture thinking, engagement, motivation, stress regulation, and the modulation of the parasympathetic nervous system (PNS).[10] This activation encourages the release of hormones like oxytocin and vasopressin, both of which promote social bonding and connection.[11]

By contrast, coaching that focuses on compliance often triggers the Negative Emotional Attractor (NEA), which is linked with the sympathetic nervous system (SNS) and releases stress-related chemicals like epinephrine and norepinephrine to prepare the body for defense. This release ultimately activates cortisol. While cortisol serves a useful function by increasing focus, it also contributes to stress and, in excess, can impair creativity and openness.

Think of it this way: Coaching with compassion is like a lighthouse that guides people safely toward growth and new possibilities, encouraging them to explore their potential. Compliance-based coaching, however, is more like a guard tower, imposing strict boundaries to keep people in line. Both approaches may achieve short-term results, but only the compassionate approach consistently fosters motivation, resilience, and adaptability.

Now, consider the critical moments in your leadership coaching conversations, feedback exchanges, and relationships. Reflect on how often you may engage the NEA rather than the PEA. Are your words and actions nurturing the positive attractor, opening the door to big-picture thinking and motivation? Or are you inadvertently pushing people into a defensive mode, limiting their perspective and stifling growth? This awareness can be a powerful tool in creating coaching environments where people feel both challenged and supported in their development.

For further insights, I recommend reading *Thinking, Fast and Slow* by Nobel Laureate Daniel Kahneman. In this book, Kahneman describes two distinct "characters" in the brain: System 1 and System 2. System 1, closely aligned with the empathic network, "operates automatically and quickly with little or no effort and no sense of voluntary control." System 2, which aligns with the analytical network, "allocates attention to the effortful mental activities that demand it, including complex computation."[12]

> This awareness can be a powerful tool in creating coaching environments where people feel both challenged and supported in their development.

Kahneman explains that we often identify most with System 2—the conscious, reasoning part of us that holds beliefs, makes choices, and decides what to think and do. Yet System 1 is what he calls "the hero of the book."[13] This framing emphasizes the importance of both systems or networks in our lives, and as coaches, we need to know how to engage them—and in what order—to maximize effectiveness.

Kahneman describes System 1 as running automatically, while System 2 typically stays in a comfortable low-effort mode. Think of System 1 as an intuitive guide, continuously generating impressions, intuitions, intentions, and feelings. System 2 is like the final editor, weighing in to approve or reject these impulses. If System 2 agrees with System 1, those impressions become beliefs, and impulses turn into deliberate actions. However, when System 1 encounters a problem it can't solve—like a navigator faced with an unexpected roadblock—it calls on System 2 to dive into deeper, more specific processing.[14]

Picture System 1 as the "autopilot" setting in an airplane: it's always running in the background, efficiently handling routine tasks. But when unexpected turbulence hits, the pilot (System 2) steps in to take control. This dynamic illustrates how both systems are essential. As coaches, we can leverage this knowledge to guide others effectively, understanding when to engage the autopilot of intuition and when to call on the reasoning power of analytical focus.

That's a lot of information to take in!

However, as coaches, it's essential for us to understand this so we can intentionally activate the brain's networks in ways that foster growth, learning, and development in those we lead. Studies using fMRI imaging show that positive, supportive approaches are more effective for helping others and driving change than negative, critical approaches. This is because positive methods activate regions of the brain that open individuals up to new ideas, while negative methods often trigger a defensive reaction, closing them down.[15]

Imagine that the brain has doors that open or close depending on how it perceives an interaction. When we approach someone with empathy, encouragement, and a growth mindset, it's like knocking on that door gently, inviting them to open up and engage.

However, a more critical or forceful approach can feel like banging on the door, causing the person to instinctively be fearful of who's on the other side, resisting opening the door to protect themselves. Our role as coaches is to know how to "knock" in a way that keeps these doors open so the individuals we coach feel safe and ready to grow.

Top NeuroCoaching Takeaways

1. **Coaches must balance the two brain networks: analytical (AN) and empathic (EN).**

   The brain has two primary networks that influence coaching effectiveness—the *analytical network* (AN) for problem-solving, data, and logic and the *empathic network* (EN) for emotional connection, creativity, and open-mindedness. Since these networks suppress each other when activated, skilled coaches must learn to *cycle between them intentionally* to foster both trust and performance.

2. **Positive coaching activates brain regions that encourage growth.**

   The fMRI research shows that coaching with compassion (the *Positive Emotional Attractor*, PEA) activates brain regions associated with creativity, motivation, and stress regulation. In contrast, coaching for compliance (the *negative emotional attractor*, NEA) triggers the brain's stress response, making individuals more defensive and resistant to change. Leaders must be mindful of which emotional response they're triggering during coaching conversations.

3. **Overusing one network leads to coaching pitfalls.**

   Too much AN (data-driven, KPI-focused coaching) can make employees feel judged. *Too much EN* (relationship-building without direction) lacks urgency or accountability for performance. Both are useful tools, but a balance is needed to create an "emotion coaster" approach—starting with empathy to open the conversation and then engaging analytical thinking to provide structure and drive results.

4. **The parasympathetic nervous system (PNS) versus sympathetic nervous system (SNS) in coaching.**

Engaging the PNS (via empathy and connection) releases oxytocin, promoting trust, relaxation, and openness to feedback. Reactivating the SNS (via stress or criticism) *triggers cortisol*, increasing focus but also creating anxiety and disengagement over time. But *sustainable coaching* can balance both, fostering motivation while maintaining psychological safety.

CHAPTER 4

THE NEUROSCIENCE OF COACHING: PART 2

Ability may get you to the top, but it takes character to keep you there.
—JOHN WOODEN

LAST YEAR, I had an incredible opportunity to speak at UCLA. As I walked across campus, something caught my eye—a sign on a building that read: "John Wooden Center Outdoor Adventure Rental Center."

I stopped in my tracks. John Wooden—a coach I deeply admire, not just for his *ten national championships* or his *eighty-eight-game winning streak*, but for the way he built relationships, fostered culture, and inspired performance. Over the years, I've had the privilege of meeting a family member and former player of Coach Wooden's, and every conversation reinforces the same truth: He *knew* his players, he *cared* about his players, and he had a rare gift—the ability to demand excellence while holding his team accountable, not to wins and losses, but to the *process*. When you consistently do the right things, day after day, wins tend to follow.

But staring at that sign, something hit me—*a revelation I had never considered.*

I love the value of adventure, and here, at an outdoor adventure rental center, was a parallel I couldn't ignore. As coaches, mentors, and leaders, we only have our people for a season. In a way, we're "renting" them for a period of time. Our job is to prepare, challenge, and equip them for whatever comes next.

> As coaches, mentors, and leaders, we only have our people for a season.

I couldn't help but wonder—what if I could discuss neuroscience and what we understand about it now with Coach Wooden? He may not have had the research at his fingertips, but make no mistake—he knew exactly how to *activate both neural networks* for motivation and learning.

The "Hand Model" of the Brain's Structure

And that brings me to another UCLA rock star: Dr. Dan Siegel. Dr. Dan Siegel of UCLA has introduced a simple way to visualize the brain's structure and functions through what he calls the "hand model" of the brain.[1] This model provides a helpful, tangible way to picture how different parts of the brain operate and interact.

Try it yourself: Start by tucking your thumb into the center of your palm. Then, wrap your four fingers over your thumb to make a fist. Your thumb should still be tucked inside. Now, let's assign each part of this hand model to a corresponding area of the brain.

In this model:

1. Your knuckles represent the cortex, the outer layer of the brain responsible for higher-order thinking, planning, and judgment.

2. Your tucked thumb represents the limbic system, the emotional center of the brain that processes feelings and memories.

3. Your palm and wrist represent the brain stem, which governs basic survival functions like breathing, heart rate, and the "fight-or-flight" response.

Use Your Hands to Imagine Your Brain

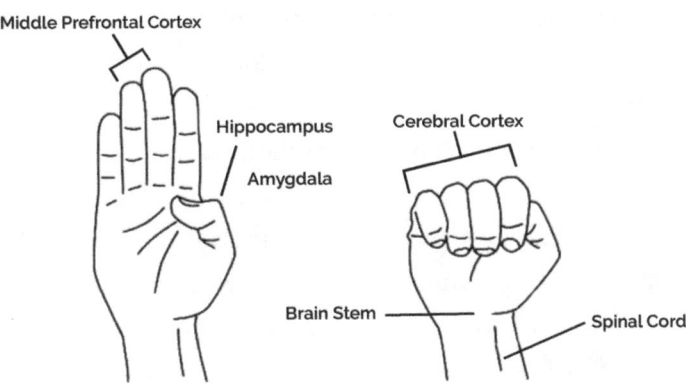

This hand model gives us a way to see how the brain is layered, from the most primitive functions in the brainstem to the complex thinking processes in the cortex. Just as your hand wraps around your thumb, the cortex wraps around and interacts with the limbic system, integrating emotions with logical thinking. It's like a team, where each part plays a role, but they're all connected.

Dr. Paul MacLean, a senior research scientist at the National Institutes of Mental Health, discovered that the human brain is made up of three distinct parts, each with specific yet interrelated functions. Dr. MacLean identified these three parts as the neocortex, the limbic system, and the root brain (r-complex).[2] Each part has its own role but also works in concert with the others, contributing to the brain's overall function and adaptability.

Now, let's return to the hand model. The palm and wrist represent the connection to the body, including the spinal cord. Dr. Siegel refers to this as the "head brain," but it's worth noting that research has shown neurons also exist around the heart and the gut, leading to the terms "heart brain" and "gut brain." While our focus is primarily on the head brain, it's fascinating to remember that these three "brains"—head, heart, and gut—often work together, influencing our reactions, decisions, and intuition.

As we go further into the hand model, I can almost picture each of you setting down this book to make a fist, following along as we explore each part. Here's a quick tour of what Dr. Siegel aimed to teach with this model. The brain stem—represented by your palm and wrist—is the oldest part of our brain, dating back over six million years. It governs the essential survival functions that keep our bodies running: digestion, circulation, breathing, heartbeat, stress response, muscle control, and balance. It's like the body's autopilot, regulating the functions we don't have to think about.

When this part of the brain is triggered, it can quickly activate our fight, flight, or freeze response. Imagine the brain stem as an ancient alarm system, ready to go off at the first sign of threat, flooding us with the instincts needed to survive. If you need a reminder of just how powerful this response can be, let me share a quick story with you.

After my oldest daughter graduated from college, she decided that her first major step into adulthood was to immediately move to New York City.

It was the summer of 2018, and I can so vividly remember moving her into the smallest apartment I've ever seen. In fact, I think I followed her around NYC for three days in a constant fight-or-flight response. There is nothing wrong with NYC, but this dad from the suburbs of Ohio was on high alert. As I walked the streets, the oldest part of my brain was hypervigilant. I will never forget the first dinner, the first walk around the city, the first subway ride, and eventually, the first time walking away from my daughter at the subway in lower Harlem to head back to the airport. If you are wondering, she did great, loved living there, and is still thriving. I am also much more comfortable in the city after all these years. Nonetheless, this is an example of the brain stem or basis of our thought process in action as a fight-or-flight response.

The Limbic System

Let's now move to the thumb, which, still tucked inside your hand, represents the limbic system. This area of the brain is responsible for regulating emotion and memory, acting as our brain's emotional "hub." Key players in the limbic system include the hippocampus (which helps us store and recall memories) and the amygdala (located right at the base of this area), which plays a central role in processing emotions, especially fear and excitement.

As we experience emotions, the limbic system connects with the body and affects our behaviors, sense of meaning, and memory formation. This part of the brain bridges the lower, survival-focused functions and the higher, logical ones, influencing our motivations, mood, and even physical sensations like pain and pleasure. Together with the root brain (r-complex), the limbic system plays a major role in activating decision-making. This area is incredibly important because it doesn't just process feelings—it shapes how we act on them.

Consider the last problem you encountered and think about how it made you feel. Did the situation evoke happiness, sadness, anger, fear, or perhaps even shame? I'd like you to take a moment to recall this problem and connect it to the emotion it stirred. Now, let's assume you didn't experience what's known as an "amygdala hijack," where the amygdala takes over, leading to an immediate, fight-or-flight response to escape the situation. Instead, you probably felt the emotion without being entirely controlled by it.

Here's an example from my experience: I was leading sales and marketing for a growing pharmaceutical company, and we were about to face a pivotal board meeting. To give you some context, this was during the 2008–2009 financial crisis. If you recall, this was a time of intense economic turmoil. The Dow Jones Industrial Average (DJIA) dropped over 1,874 points, or 18 percent, from October 6 to October 10, 2008. These were unprecedented losses.

As the recession took hold, the United States lost over 8.7 million jobs (according to the US Bureau of Labor Statistics),[3] doubling the unemployment rate. According to the US Department of the Treasury, US households lost approximately $17 trillion in net worth as the stock market plummeted,[4] largely due to the collapse of mortgage-backed securities tied to American real estate.[5] I provide these details to paint a clear picture of the immense stress and high emotions that filled the room as my board of directors and I prepared for this meeting.

In this environment, everyone's limbic system was likely on high alert, feeding intense emotions of fear, urgency, and uncertainty into our thoughts and decisions. The limbic system was fully engaged, influencing not only how we felt but also how we approached the challenges ahead.

At this point, our organization had roughly $300 million of venture capital invested in developing two new drugs, acquiring a bolt-on company, and building a full-scale sales and marketing infrastructure to launch these products. Before the market crash, everything was on track: Both drugs were nearing approval, we had hired around 250 people for our commercial organization, we'd held a launch meeting for a new product, and we were steadily establishing our presence across the United States. Then, the market crashed. The product launch stalled due to reimbursement challenges; we couldn't take the company public, and the board's anxiety understandably grew.

For context, an SEC Form S-1 is a registration requirement for US companies that want to be publicly listed on a national exchange. During the recession, keeping the S-1 active with Morgan Stanley was costing us millions. Eventually, we had no choice but to pull it. To say the least, this was a challenging situation.

As we entered the boardroom, it was clear we had tough decisions to make. One was whether to take down the S-1 filing, which we ultimately did. Another was whether to dismantle the salesforce just one year after we had built it from the ground up—a decision the company ultimately made. Let's take a moment to revisit the neurochemistry at play in this high-stress scenario.

While I couldn't physically flee the boardroom, my "root brain" was certainly on high alert, triggering intense emotions like fear, anxiety, anger, and sadness that filled my mind. My limbic system—the emotional core of my brain—was fully activated. If I'd been hooked up to a fMRI at that moment, I'm certain that the areas of my brain represented in the hand model (especially the thumb, representing the limbic system) would have been lighting up like a Christmas tree. This experience provides a powerful example of how emotions and stress influence our decision-making processes.

The stress was so overwhelming that my central nervous system felt overloaded. It was as if my entire body had shifted into a state of emergency, preparing to tackle a threat that, in this case, wasn't a physical danger but a deeply personal and professional one. In the months that followed, the market didn't improve, public offerings remained rare, the organization reduced its field team, and eventually, the products were sold to other companies. The story didn't end as we had hoped, but this is the reality of business.

I share this example because, as leader/coaches, we must recognize that our brain chemistry has a direct impact on how we lead, especially under stress. The brain's reactions to challenging situations don't just influence our personal feelings—they shape our decisions and, by extension, our organization's path forward.

Now, consider your own example. How did your situation unfold, and what emotions were triggered for you? This awareness of your emotional state and neurochemical response can offer valuable insights into how you might approach future high-stress decisions.

The Prefrontal Cortex

Now, let's close our fist and focus on the part of the brain represented by our knuckles. This area corresponds to the cortex. Dr. Siegel describes the cortex as the part of the brain where we "make maps of the world."[6] It's here that our conscious thought processes unfold—where we analyze facts, process information logically, interpret sensory inputs, and make judgments.

If you look closely at the lowest set of knuckles near your fingernails, this area represents the prefrontal cortex, where higher-level integration occurs. This part of the brain connects and synthesizes information from other areas, allowing you to make thoughtful decisions rather than reacting impulsively. Soon, we'll discuss how this area works with other parts of the brain to validate and guide decision-making.

So how does all this affect trust in our relationships? I often pose this question to audiences and training groups: *How long does it take to build trust?* And *how long does it take to damage trust?* Answers may vary, but a universal truth emerges: It takes far longer to build trust than to break it. Trust is like constructing a house with a solid foundation—it can take months or years to build, yet one powerful storm can level it in an instant. Whether we live in a small, modest space or a multi-million-dollar mansion, the fragility of trust remains the same.

> It takes far longer to build trust than to break it.

In our relationships, the same principle applies. To truly build trust, we need to know how to authentically engage our neurochemistry, fostering connections that feel real and reliable. This approach not only strengthens relationships but also drives performance. However, I feel it's important to include a word of caution here: The more we understand neurochemistry, the greater the risk of misusing this knowledge. Understanding neurochemistry in coaching should be about facilitating growth, not manipulating others.

There's a fine line between modulating neurochemistry for positive impact and using it to control or exploit people's responses. As coaches, we must be mindful of this line. Manipulation has no place in genuine coaching. True leadership is grounded in connection and trust, and any use of neurochemistry should be aimed at supporting others, not exerting undue influence.

If you take a moment, I'm sure you can think of a few leaders who have used charisma and manipulation to influence others, whether in your own life or from broader examples. It's a powerful reminder that if we're striving to lead with connection and trust, we should begin by clearly defining what trust really means.

There are both personal and professional trust elements. On the personal trust elements, we see words like vulnerability, honesty, authenticity, and humility. On the professional trust elements, we see words like knowledge, capabilities, and insights. We refer to the following picture as the Periodic Table of Trust. As you reflect on these elements, challenge yourself as to how you, as a coach, leverage these elements in your situational moments of impact.

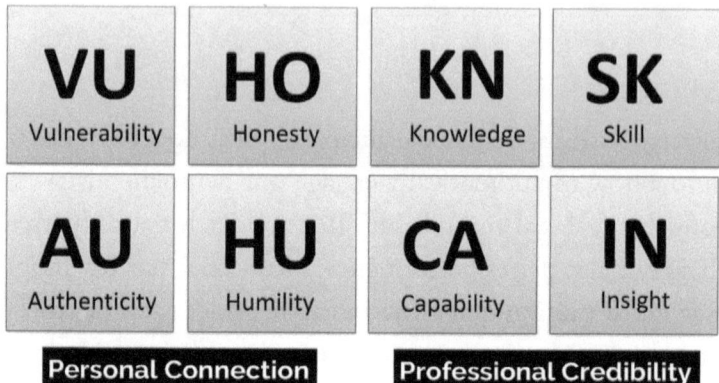

In her book *Dare to Lead*, Brené Brown—widely known for her work on vulnerability—references research by John Gottman, who has spent forty years studying intimate relationships.[7] Gottman describes how trust is built in what he calls "sliding door" moments, inspired by the movie *Sliding Doors*. He explains, "What I've found through research is that trust is built in very small moments, which I call 'sliding door' moments. In any interaction, there is a possibility of connecting with your partner or turning away from your partner."[8] Each of these small, seemingly insignificant moments is an opportunity to build or weaken trust, depending on whether we choose to engage or withdraw.

With this in mind, consider the importance of Brown's observation that trust is "the stacking and layering of small moments and reciprocal vulnerability over time."[9] Trust isn't typically built in grand gestures; instead, it accumulates through repeated acts of openness and responsiveness, creating a foundation that grows stronger with each interaction. Think of trust as a series of bricks that, when stacked carefully over time, form a solid wall. Remove just one brick, and the structure remains strong, but remove too many, and the wall becomes unstable.

Before we go further, let's consider Brené Brown's definition of vulnerability. She and her team describe vulnerability as "the emotion that we experience during times of uncertainty, risk, and emotional exposure. Vulnerability is not winning or losing; it's having the courage to show up when you can't control the outcome."[10] This definition helps illustrate why vulnerability is so essential to building personal connection. Far from being a weakness, vulnerability is a strength—it's the courage to engage fully, even when the stakes are high and the outcome is uncertain.

Brown's research reinforces this view: "Across all of our data, there's not a shred of empirical evidence that vulnerability is weakness."[11] In fact, it's quite the opposite. By allowing ourselves to be vulnerable, we invite trust and openness, creating an environment where meaningful connection can flourish. Vulnerability, therefore, is not a liability in relationships; it's the key to authentic connection.

> Far from being a weakness, vulnerability is a strength—it's the courage to engage fully, even when the stakes are high and the outcome is uncertain.

Take a moment and reflect on how you show up in coaching conversations. Do you show up leading with professional credibility or personal connection? If I asked which is more important, how would you respond? As I've been stating in this chapter, both are equally as important. Think about how you authentically leverage both in coaching conversations and in which order.

In his book *The Neuroscience of Trust*, Paul Zak reports that building a culture of trust is a key differentiator in organizations. Employees in high-trust environments are more productive, have more energy, collaborate better, and are more likely to stay with their employers.[12] Zak's research team conducted experiments over a decade to identify what promotes and inhibits oxytocin, the "bonding hormone." They discovered that high stress significantly inhibits oxytocin, while the presence of oxytocin increases empathy.[13] Through experiments and surveys, Zak identified eight management behaviors that foster trust: (1) recognition, (2) induced challenge stress, (3) intentional relationship-building, (4) facilitation of whole-person growth, (5) allowing discretion in how people perform their jobs, (6) enabling job crafting, (7) broad sharing of information, and (8) showing vulnerability.[14]

This balance between cortisol and oxytocin highlights the importance of neurochemical homeostasis. According to Social Self-Preservation Theory, situations that threaten one's social value can trigger issues related to self-esteem and elevate cortisol levels.[15] When cortisol is triggered, the sympathetic nervous system activates, often resulting in feelings of shame and reduced self-esteem, particularly in evaluative situations. Imagine cortisol as a "stress shield" that goes up, shutting down social openness in an effort to protect against perceived threats.

Again, this is a lot of scientific information!

I'd love to tell you that I've always fully understood the brain science behind these insights, but that wouldn't be true. The reality of leadership is that most people don't explore this knowledge in depth. I spent over twenty years in the pharmaceutical industry (primarily focused on neuroscience), yet I never gave much thought to how the brain's biology, physiology, and psychology directly impact decision-making. I feel deeply compelled to share this knowledge with you because I believe it's valuable for every role you may hold—as a friend, parent, coach, teacher, counselor, or manager.

When you go into a coaching conversation, you need to think about these areas of the brain as we have defined them in this chapter. If you take the hand model, you are thinking about and activating them from the "inside out" in your coaching conversations. Said another way, think about the wrist, palm, thumb, and knuckles. As we describe in the companion sales book, NeuroSelling®, "engage with the instinctive brain, then work up to the feeling brain, then—and only then—coach to the skeptical brain."[16] Inside out coaching is a fundamental belief in our approach to NeuroCoaching.

To bring this back to a personal level, when my wife and I were deciding whether to adopt our youngest daughter, this decision obviously stirred up tremendous emotions. Once we activated the decision-making process, we immediately began seeking facts, figures, and data to support our choice. At that moment, our cortex—the thinking brain—was fully engaged, analyzing the information. Thankfully, this combination of emotion and logic helped us make one of the best decisions of our lives.

Top NeuroCoaching Takeaways

1. **Balance empathy and analysis in coaching.**

   The most effective coaches know how to engage both empathic and analytical brain networks in coaching conversations. By balancing empathy and analysis, coaches can create an environment that fosters connection while providing direction. This dual activation helps team members feel both supported and challenged, paving the way for meaningful growth and commitment to change.

2. **Understand and use "sliding door" moments.**

   Trust is built through small, intentional actions over time. Every interaction—no matter how small—offers a "sliding door" moment to either connect with or distance from those you lead. Being conscious of these moments and showing consistent empathy and support will layer trust, strengthening relationships and increasing long-term engagement.

3. **Use the "emotion coaster" technique.**

   Enter challenging conversations by first engaging the empathic network to create openness. Then, shift to the analytical network to discuss facts and goals. This "emotion coaster" approach enables a coach to avoid overloading either network, leading to more balanced and impactful conversations that encourage positive change without creating resistance.

4. **Recognize and modulate the stress response in coaching.**

   High-stress environments inhibit oxytocin and activate cortisol, which can lead to defensiveness, reduced creativity, and impaired problem-solving. Recognize when a coaching situation may be increasing stress and intentionally adjust to a more supportive tone to reduce cortisol. By doing so, you help your team members stay open to learning, growth, and adaptation.

5. **Create a culture of psychological safety and autonomy.**

    Leadership behaviors that build trust—such as recognition, autonomy, vulnerability, and shared information—foster a culture where employees feel safe and valued. Psychological safety allows individuals to take risks, learn from mistakes, and engage more deeply, ultimately enhancing productivity and retention. Leaders who model these behaviors create an environment that naturally supports personal and professional growth.

CHAPTER 5

NEUROVISIONING

Vision is a picture of the future that produces passion.
—Bill Hybels

WE'VE ALWAYS HAD a clear vision for Braintrust—to build a company focused on improving lives by improving the way people communicate using the power of neuroscience and behavioral psychology. I also knew that our "lane" would be in sales, leadership, and coaching. We created very innovative and interactive live workshops that took interesting research (*information*) and translated it into clear *application*. Little did I know a once-in-a-century event would test that vision in more ways than I had imagined. Yes, like the rest of the world, we were confronted with the first global pandemic since the early twentieth century. As everyone adapted to isolation, familiarizing themselves with DoorDash, trying to navigate the complexities of homeschooling on Zoom, and determining whether or not they were able to turn their camera on and unmute themselves for the latest conference call, we found ourselves in a frenzy to overhaul our business model, previously 90 percent reliant on live, in-person engagements.

Enter Ingvar Kamprad. His is not a name that easily rolls off the tongue or garners instant familiarity. Well, Ingvar also had a vision for his company, one that started in 1943 when he began selling small pens and wallets by mail order at the age of seventeen from a small farm called Elmtaryd outside the nearby village of Agunnard in Sweden. His first major transformation occurred in 1948 when he began selling furniture. This marked a shift toward larger household items, laying the foundation for Ingvar's future as a furniture retailer.

In the 1950s, his company revolutionized the furniture market with the introduction of flat-pack furniture, a move that cut costs, minimized damage during shipping, saved on storage, and simplified transport for customers. This innovation required a sweeping overhaul of operations, from design to logistics, necessitating a flexible and adaptive approach from the team, but it was a vision that catapulted his company to the forefront of the industry. You've likely made the connection by now that his company is IKEA. And the origin of the name? It's an acronym: "I" (for Ingvar), "K" (Kamprad), "E" (Elmtaryd, the family farm), and "A" (Agunnaryd, the village).[1]

So what does Braintrust's vision have in common with that of IKEA? Standing amidst an array of "flat-packed" boxes, I couldn't help but laugh at the serendipity. Ingvar's dream of bringing affordable furniture to the masses dovetailed with my mission to outfit new studios for virtual training and coaching. Yes, my relationship with Ingvar is bittersweet. On the one hand, I'm grateful for the ability to swiftly create professional-looking backdrops for our sessions, enhancing the visual appeal for our trainers and coaches. On the other, the hours spent deciphering what felt like ancient hieroglyphics in the assembly manuals, trying to coax Part A into aligning with Part B—when Part A seemed to have developed a personal vendetta against Part B—were nothing short of exasperating. Yet, as any intrepid soul who has embarked on the IKEA furniture assembly odyssey knows, after a series of negotiations, a little bit of muscle, and perhaps a few choice words, you emerge victorious. With a bookshelf standing strong, add a couple of strategically placed lights, a high-quality camera, and presto: You've transformed a pile of panels and screws into a sleek, professional virtual studio. Our vision held true and never faltered, even as our business transformed overnight. It's due to the *shared vision* our company has at the organization, leader, and employee levels that not only kept us all rowing in the same direction during a pandemic but also helped us grow even faster and more efficiently in that same direction.

In the journey of transforming an organization from good to great or steering a startup toward its beacon of success, there's one element that stands as both the compass and the North Star: *vision*. As I've navigated through the depths of leadership and organizational development, the conversations always circle back to vision—how a clear, compelling vision can drive an organization forward or the absence of it can lead to its downfall. But what if we could dive deeper into the mechanics of vision? What if we could unlock the secrets of how vision is formed, communicated, and shared, not just on a psychological level but through the lens of neuroscience?

The concept of vision in business is nothing new. It's been discussed, dissected, and debated across boardrooms and bestsellers for decades. Yet what we often overlook is the profound impact of neuroscience on understanding and leveraging vision within our organizations. Neuroscience offers us unprecedented insights into how our brains perceive, process, and pursue vision. It's where the intangible meets the tangible, where the art of visioning intersects with the science of application.

The Power of a Shared Vision

As someone who has consulted with companies from the Fortune 500 down to small businesses and written multiple books on the subject, I've seen firsthand the power of applying neuroscience to enhance strategies that improve communication. Now, we turn our focus to the *organizational vision*—exploring how neuroscience can illuminate the path to shared success. Through this exploration, we lean into the science of company vision, translating these insights into leadership practices and operational strategies, ultimately fostering a deeper understanding and alignment of the vision of every employee.

Why is this important? Because in a world that's rapidly changing, where businesses must adapt and evolve at an unprecedented pace, a shared vision is the anchor that keeps us grounded. It's what motivates us to push forward, innovate, and achieve our collective goals. Neuroscience provides us with a road map to understanding how to create, communicate, and cultivate this shared vision more effectively.

> A shared vision is the anchor that keeps us grounded. It's what motivates us to push forward, innovate, and achieve our collective goals.

So let's discover how the principles of neuroscience can lead us to a clearer, more compelling vision for our organizations—a vision that doesn't just exist in the minds of a few but is shared, embraced, and pursued by every single person who is part of the journey.

At the heart of every groundbreaking achievement and thriving organization is a powerful, compelling vision. But where does this vision originate? It's not in the boardrooms or brainstorming sessions but within the intricate neural networks of our minds. Neuroscience has unveiled that vision forms in the empathic network in constant dialogue with our emotions, memories, and experiences stored across various brain regions (as we discussed in prior chapters). When we talk about a company vision, we're activating more than just the logical parts of our brain; we're tapping into our deepest hopes, fears, and aspirations. It's a symphony of neural activity where emotion and logic intertwine, giving birth to something that's both a dream and a directive. Understanding this neural basis of vision creation is crucial. It tells us that crafting a company vision isn't just about defining business goals; it's about connecting with the very core of what makes us human.

> When leaders articulate a vision in a way that resonates on a personal level, they're essentially priming their teams' brains for action, setting the stage for collective achievement.

But how does a vision, once formed, inspire action and drive motivation? Here, the limbic system plays a starring role, particularly the dopamine pathways associated with reward and pleasure. When employees can see how their efforts contribute to achieving the company vision, their brains release dopamine, not just at the achievement of the goal but in anticipation of it. This not only boosts motivation but also reinforces the behavior needed to pursue that vision. This neurochemical process underlines the importance of clearly communicating the company vision and making it tangible. It's not enough for the vision to be inspiring; it must be visible, felt, and believed by everyone in the organization. When leaders articulate a vision in a way that resonates on a personal level, they're essentially priming their teams' brains for action, setting the stage for collective achievement.

The power of a *shared* vision lies in its ability to synchronize a group's intentions and actions toward a common purpose, leading to higher goal achievement. This phenomenon, from a neuroscientific perspective, can be likened to mirror neurons at work. These neurons, which fire both when an individual acts and when they observe the same action performed by another, are foundational to empathy and understanding. In the context of a company vision, they facilitate a shared emotional and motivational state across the organization. This neural mirroring doesn't just enhance cohesion; it amplifies the vision's impact. When individuals see their leaders and peers aligned with the company vision, it reinforces their own commitment and motivation. This collective neural engagement creates a powerful ripple effect, propelling the organization toward its vision with a unified force.

In this exploration of the science behind vision, we see that vision isn't merely a business tool; it's a deeply human one rooted in the neural fabric of our beings. By understanding and leveraging the neuroscience of vision, leaders can craft a vision that resonates on a deeper level, driving motivation, action, and, ultimately, shared success. This section underscores the need for a vision that's not only ambitious but also deeply human, capable of touching the hearts and minds of everyone involved.

The Leader's Brain on Vision

Leadership and neuroscience converge in a fascinating landscape of potential and purpose. Empathy (critical in emotional intelligence), largely governed by another part of the brain called the anterior insula, plays a crucial role in leadership vision. It allows leaders to understand and share their team's feelings, creating a vision that resonates on a personal level with each member. This neural engagement promotes a deeper connection between the leader's vision and the team's aspirations, driving collective motivation and commitment.

Communicating Vision

The act of communicating a vision is, in essence, a neural symphony where words, emotions, and visions converge. Neuroscience shows us that stories are not just tales; they are experiences that our brains live through. When leaders share their vision through storytelling, they're engaging the listener's brain as if it were experiencing the vision firsthand. This is due to the brain's default mode network (also known as the empathic network), which is activated during storytelling and helps in creating personal connections with the narrative.

Moreover, effective communication of a vision leverages emotional resonance, tapping into the limbic system's power to bind memories and emotions. Leaders who can articulate their vision in a way that strikes an emotional chord will find their vision not just understood but felt. This emotional engagement ensures that the vision is remembered and acted upon, deeply embedding it within the organization's collective psyche.

Inspiring Others

To inspire is to literally "breathe life into." This is what leaders do when they successfully inspire their teams toward a vision. The neuroscience behind inspiration involves a complex interplay of neural circuits, including those related to reward (dopamine), social connection (oxytocin), and empathy (mirror neurons). When leaders inspire, they're not just directing; they're connecting, engaging, and energizing their teams on a neural level.

Inspiring leadership involves more than just charisma. It requires authenticity, vulnerability, and the ability to connect with others' dreams and aspirations. Leaders who can share their vision with genuine passion and openness create an environment where inspiration flourishes. This environment nurtures the neural conditions necessary for motivation, creativity, and commitment to soar.

The best coaches understand how to optimize neurotransmitters to create a coaching experience that fosters trust (oxytocin), motivation (dopamine), confidence (serotonin), stress resilience (endorphins), and psychological safety (managing cortisol). By leveraging neuroscience, coaches can enhance connection and credibility, leading to more impactful and lasting results.

Vision-Driven Decision-Making

At the intersection of vision and action lies the critical process of decision-making. Neuroscience teaches us that effective decision-making, especially under the guidance of a clear vision, involves a complex dance between the analytical network (AN) and the empathic network (EN). This neural interplay balances logical analysis with emotional intuition, guiding leaders in making choices that not only align with the company's goals but also resonate with the collective emotional landscape of their teams.

For a vision to transcend the realm of ideas and manifest in the daily operations of an organization, it must be embedded in every decision, from the strategic to the mundane. Leaders and managers equipped with an understanding of their own neural decision-making processes can more adeptly align their choices with the overarching vision, ensuring consistency and coherence in action. This alignment is not just about adherence to goals but about nurturing a decision-making culture that embodies the vision at every level.

Cultivating a Visionary Culture

The culture of an organization is its heartbeat, the living, breathing manifestation of its values and visions. Cultivating a visionary culture means creating an environment where the brain's natural tendencies toward social cohesion and mimicry work in favor of the organizational vision. Neuroscience shows us that human brains are wired to align with the group's norms and values, a tendency rooted in our evolutionary need for social belonging. Leaders can leverage this neural predisposition by embodying the vision in their behavior, setting a neurobiological precedent for others to follow.

When Satya Nadella took over as CEO of Microsoft, he didn't just preach a culture of growth and collaboration—he modeled it by actively engaging in technical learning, shifting mindsets through his own behavior. This process involves more than just leading by example; it requires conscious effort to create narratives, rituals, and symbols that reinforce the vision at every touchpoint. At Ritz-Carlton, for instance, employees participate in daily "lineup" meetings to share exceptional customer service stories, embedding the company's service philosophy into their neural pathways through repetition and shared experience. Toyota's Kaizen approach further illustrates this, where even frontline workers are encouraged to contribute ideas for improvement, fostering an environment where employees instinctively align their behaviors with the company's commitment to continuous growth.

Such a culture not only supports the operationalization of the vision but also strengthens the neural connections associated with these visionary ideals, making the vision a lived experience for every member of the organization.

Neuroplasticity and Adaptation

The brain's ability to adapt and reorganize itself, known as neuroplasticity, is perhaps its most miraculous feature. In the context of implementing an operating vision, neuroplasticity offers a beacon of hope and a tool for transformation. As organizations evolve, so must their visions. Leaders who understand neuroplasticity recognize the importance of continuously engaging their teams in new learning and experiences, aligning these activities with the evolving vision.

> As organizations evolve, so must their visions.

This adaptive approach allows an organization to remain agile, responsive to changes in the external environment, and aligned internally with a shared sense of purpose. It involves not just the top-down communication of vision changes but also fostering an environment where feedback, innovation, and ideation are encouraged, allowing the organizational vision to be shaped and reshaped by the collective intelligence and creativity of its people.

As we lead to a deeper dive into shared vision, Coach Bill Belichick, six-time Superbowl champion, stated that "you need that shared vision between ownership and coaching and scouting, and that's when you can be successful... I had that up until about the last four years in New England. And when you have that shared vision and everybody pulling in the same direction, you have a chance, and you can get a lot done. And even if you don't win at all, you're still really competitive... but when you're going in different directions, then that makes it really hard to keep up with everybody else."[2] Whether you're a Coach Belichick fan or not, he reminds us of the importance of shared vision—a critical foundational piece of the sustained performance puzzle.

Top NeuroCoaching Takeaways

1. **Neuroscience explains why vision drives action.**

   As discussed, a vision is deeply embedded in psychology and neuroscience. Our brain's emotional and reward systems play key roles in motivation and engagement. So when employees connect emotionally with a company's vision, they're more likely to actively commit and pursue it.

2. **Leadership communication shapes vision adoption.**

   Shaping visions isn't just about defining goals; it's about *how* leaders communicate them. Storytelling, emotional resonance, and mirroring through leadership behavior activate neural processes that enhance motivation and alignment.

3. **Culture reinforces and sustains vision.**

   A strong vision must be embedded in the culture through daily rituals, behaviors, and decision-making processes. Leaders must actively shape and model a visionary culture in order to ensure long-term alignment.

CHAPTER 6

SHARED VISION

I wanna build something that's gonna outlive me.
—Lin-Manuel Miranda's Hamilton

IMAGINE WALKING INTO a workplace where everyone—leaders, teams, and individuals—moves in sync, driven by a shared sense of purpose. A workplace is not just about hitting targets or following processes; it's about something deeper—an alignment of vision, values, and aspirations that fosters trust, fuels motivation, and transforms the way people work together.

As discussed in our prior chapter, shared vision is the foundation of meaningful leadership. It's the bridge between an organization's mission and the daily actions of its people. In this chapter, we'll explore how aligning organizational, leadership, and employee vision and values creates a relational foundation—one that strengthens trust and builds deeper, more impactful relationships.

But vision alone is not enough. Great leaders understand that coaching is a dynamic balance between relationships and results. Shared vision must be coupled with an aligned mission to achieve relational and operational excellence. It's not about choosing between connection, credibility, and performance—it's about mastering both through communication. There is no more powerful gift we can give as leaders than the ability to be a world-class communicator.

Let's look at our coaching journey through the lens of a mountain climber. As a side note, I've always been fascinated by Mt. Everest. I guess it is the adventurer in me. This time, the mountain we'll be climbing is communication excellence in our coaching.

Climbing the mountain of communication is no less treacherous than summiting Everest. As any mountaineer knows, the path to the top is filled with unexpected weather, shifting terrain, and the ominous "death zone"—a place where oxygen thins and decisions become life or death. In coaching, we face our own death zone, what we call the ICU: the *intensive conversation unit*. It's where communication can break down, trust can falter, and progress can stall. But with the right approach, the summit is within reach. Our ascent begins with *shared vision*—the basecamp of clarity—where we align vision and values at the organizational, leader, and employee levels. From there, we climb toward *aligned mission*, anchoring ourselves to strategy, standards, and strengths. And finally, we navigate the ever-changing ridge lines of *situational conversations*, where we assess six key intersections—purpose, perspective, plan/path, progress, problems, and performance. Together, these three steps form the foundation for a strong coaching climate—one that fosters deeper relationships, open dialogue, and elevated engagement and performance. Welcome to the heart of Neurocoaching.

Shared Vision
+ Aligned Mission
+ Situational Conversations
= Coaching Climate

THE NEUROCOACHING FORMULA

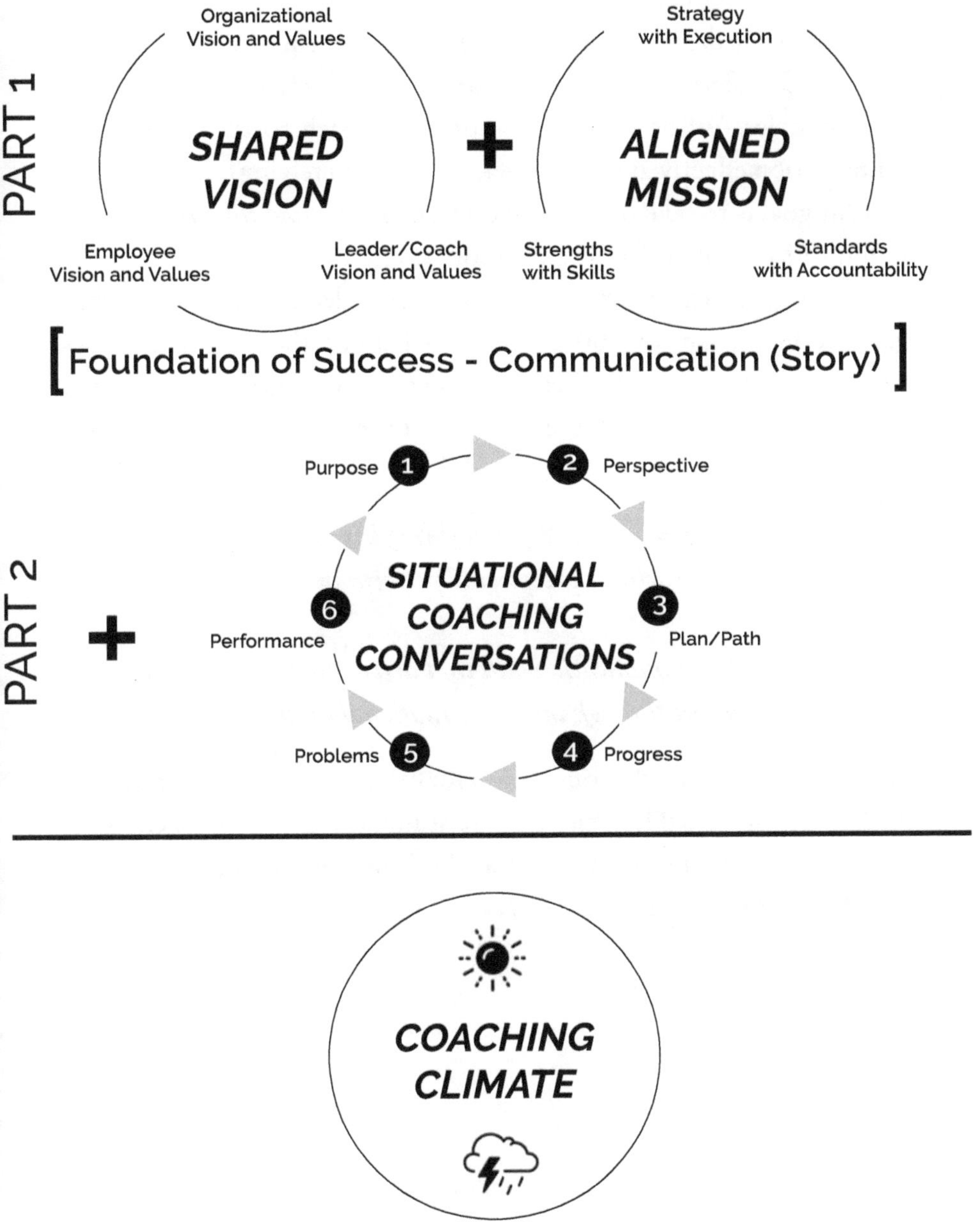

PART 1

SHARED VISION
- Organizational Vision and Values
- Employee Vision and Values
- Leader/Coach Vision and Values

+

ALIGNED MISSION
- Strategy with Execution
- Strengths with Skills
- Standards with Accountability

[Foundation of Success - Communication (Story)]

PART 2

+

SITUATIONAL COACHING CONVERSATIONS
1. Purpose
2. Perspective
3. Plan/Path
4. Progress
5. Problems
6. Performance

COACHING CLIMATE

As any mountaineer will tell you, this process is a journey, and we will have setbacks.

When these three elements come together, leaders are positioned to create a flourishing coaching climate. In later chapters, we will explore what amplifies or dampens that climate, including emotional intelligence, psychological safety, thoughtful questioning, active listening, and leadership styles. Without a foundational approach to the mountain of communication effectiveness, however, we are often relying on our intuitive skills. Our goal is to take the intuitive and make it more *intentional* in our communication toolset. Communication discipline is a strength.

We can't go on this journey without defining leadership and coaching. If we were in a room of 100 people and I asked them to define these terms, we would have 100 different answers; however, the following are the working definitions we've established over thousands of leadership coaching sessions:

Leadership = inspiring others through a shared vision to achieve exceptional performance

Coaching = a communication skill that drives sustained growth & performance through tailored situational conversations

These definitions set the foundation for our journey. Let's start by going to the field for an actual life sciences case study where NeuroCoaching was implemented over a multi-year period. Let's put on our mountaineering backpacks filled with our essential gear and begin the adventure!

NEUROCOACHING Playbook

A Case Study in Leadership Transformation

The Call That Changed Everything

In 2022, Jeff and I were speaking at a leadership experience hosted at the National Football League Hall of Fame (what a thrill to be there)—a fitting place for breakthrough moments, surrounded by coaching legends. Amid that experience, we received a call from a life sciences executive facing a critical challenge:

- Their leaders needed to coach with greater impact.
- Their sales professionals needed to communicate more effectively with customers.

This wasn't just another coaching initiative. The company needed real transformation, and after reading an article we had written on using communication to lead through change, they reached out to us. That moment set everything in motion.

The NeuroCoaching Playbook: Pillars of Transformation

Once we partnered with this incredible company, we had a realization—a tipping point. After decades of coaching, research, and refining our methodology, we knew that NeuroCoaching was about to change everything for this team.

Our approach centered on three critical pillars:

Shared Vision + Aligned Mission

Aligning values, vision, strategy, standards, and strengths
at the *organizational, team,* and *individual* levels
to create a compelling coaching vision.

Situational Conversations

Equipping leaders with the tools
to navigate coaching conversations effectively,
using a decision-based framework
to drive clarity and accountability.

Coaching Climate

Establishing a sustainable culture of coaching through
emotional intelligence, psychological safety, questioning,
active listening, and leadership styles.

The Breakthrough Training That Redefined Leadership

Let's step into this company, based in a Chicago suburban office, where fifty experienced leaders engaged in a two-day NeuroCoaching training. These weren't just role-play exercises—these were *real coaching scenarios* designed to challenge and elevate their leadership coaching approach.

As they paired up, working through situational conversations, the room transformed. Leaders who previously struggled to engage in high-impact coaching began unlocking insights, asking better questions, and shifting their approach. That was the moment we knew—NeuroCoaching wasn't just theory; it was a game-changer in action.

The Lasting Impact: The Numbers Speak for Themselves

Over the next several years, our partnership with this organization led to *measurable, lasting change*:

- ✓ *Engagement increased* as leaders gained confidence in coaching.
- ✓ *Productivity improved* as teams aligned around a shared vision and situational coaching excellence.
- ✓ *Turnover dropped from 25 percent to just 5 percent*, proving that leaders who coach effectively create an environment where people want to stay and grow.
- ✓ *Hundreds of professionals* across multiple levels experienced transformation through improved coaching conversations.

This case study is a testament to how *NeuroCoaching fuels individual, leader, and team growth*, leading to sustainable performance outcomes.

Shared Vision: The Foundation of Coaching Success

As we continue this journey, let's explore the first and most foundational component of NeuroCoaching: *shared vision*—how aligning values and vision creates a coaching foundation that drives sustained results.

The shared vision approach isn't just about putting words on a page; we as leaders have to *communicate* and *live* that vision to create a world-class climate. The world's most effective leader/coaches are authentic storytellers who root their approach so deeply in the ground that it allows the team to adapt, survive, and thrive in moments of change.

The NeuroCoaching framework you are about to learn and apply is both empirically supported and practically relevant. We knew we could finally put this work into your hands (three years after launch) once we surpassed thousands of leader/coaches who have utilized it. Now that we've crossed that milestone, it's time to equip you with the tools to create high-impact coaching conversations that lead to sustained performance.

Coaching with Compassion – A Journey-Altering Assignment

Back when I first embarked on my PhD journey, there was one course that stood out—DM613: Leading Change, taught by Dr. Richard Boyatzis. As we learned in Chapter 3, he's a giant in the field of leadership, emotional intelligence, and behavior change. He's a professor, author, and researcher whose work has transformed leadership, coaching, relationships, and sustained change.

Early in the course, I remember asking him: "Isn't a lot of what we're learning just common sense?"

His response was profound:

"What is common sense is NOT often common practice."

That idea stuck with me. We often know what we should do, but without intentionality, we don't consistently apply it.

Boyatzis co-authored *Primal Leadership* with Daniel Goleman and Annie McKee, a book that's become a cornerstone within my study of leadership and emotional intelligence. It introduced the concept of resonant leadership and emphasized the importance of emotional intelligence in leadership effectiveness. This book had such an impact that I've had over 800 students read it at both the undergraduate and graduate levels.

Back to that first class, Leading Change. As I reviewed the syllabus, I noticed that we had to complete several exercises throughout the semester—a *personal vision* project and a *coaching with compassion* project. The coaching with compassion had to be done with a current executive, where we assessed an intentional change effort and the role of leadership at multiple levels.

For the coaching with compassion assignment, I needed to interview a leader and put them into the PEA (Positive Emotional Attractor) mindset, then authentically attempt to keep the leader in that state for an hour. If the conversation started to move to the NEA (Negative Emotional Attractor), we had to work to redirect through questions and active listening.

I interviewed the chief transformation officer of a Fortune 100 company—someone I had never met—with the goal of practicing coaching with compassion in a one-hour coaching session. This involved discussing the person's dreams, aspirations, hopes, values, and story. I was guided by a series of questions to assist with the interview:

1. If your life were perfect and your dreams came true, what would your life and work be like in ten to fifteen years?

2. What are the values or virtues that are most important to you?

3. What kind of person would you love to be?

4. Who helped you the most to become who you are or get to where you are?

5. What would you wish your legacy to be?

To be honest, I thought this exercise was crazy and a waste of time. However, what happened next changed the trajectory of my program and leadership journey. When I asked that first question, my interviewee turned away from her computer, looked out the window, took a huge breath, relaxed her shoulders, and said, "No one has ever asked me that question."

At that moment, I realized what it meant to put someone authentically into a PEA state. We had the most amazing conversation, where I learned about her dreams, hopes, aspirations, and so much more. After the session, I went to my car, closed the door, and, with tears in my eyes, vividly remembered thinking this:

How is it that I know more in one hour about someone I had never met than I do about team members who have worked for me for more than five years?

These projects opened my eyes to my passion area of research, which is leader–team member relationships. After isolating this focus, I became even more aware that the 1:1 relationships also impact multiple levels within teams, organizations, and society. Two of these exercises helped inform my research journey, my academic journey, and now our consulting practice at Braintrust and the eventual co-creation of NeuroCoaching.

Shared vision is more than a concept—it's a framework for meaningful leadership. In our opinion, it is a nonnegotiable for you as a leader. It fosters a sense of belonging, social identity, and the internalization of values that drive high-quality relationships. Research by Boyatzis, Rochford, and Taylor shared in *Frontiers in Psychology* supports this: "The role of the Positive Emotional Attractor in vision and shared vision: toward effective leadership, relationships, and engagement."[1] For vision to create lasting change, it must be rooted in an ideal self and reinforced through a positive emotional state.

In their article, the authors made three key arguments:

1. A personal vision based on an ideal self (who you desire to be) is required if the vision is to lead to sustained and desired change.

2. To create a personal vision based on an ideal self—or, among others, a shared vision—a person must be in the PEA (Positive Emotional Attractor).

3. While the NEA (Negative Emotional Attractor) is required to move a person from vision to action, a person must spend significantly more time in the PEA to achieve sustained desired change.

A shared vision creates a sense of belonging, social identity, and internalization of values and attitudes—all of which are characteristics of high-quality relationships.[2] The presence of a shared vision suggests that the relationships incorporated within a given dyad (leader–team member) have moved beyond our initial basic needs to be liked and to belong[3] to more profound, meaningful, and sustainable bonds.

Leadership carries with it the responsibility of being forward-looking, the ability to see beyond the immediate horizon to imagine and articulate a future brimming with possibilities. Bailey and Madden, in their work "What Makes Work Meaningful—Or Meaningless," highlight the significance of envisioning a positive future that imbues work with a profound sense of meaning and purpose.[4] This vision, when shared, has the power to attract more people, fuel intrinsic motivation, and withstand myriad challenges, as discussed by Kouzes and Posner in *Everyday People, Extraordinary Leadership*.[5]

The Importance of a Shared Vision and Shared Values

A foundational vision and values are crucial for impacting performance, entailing a journey of self-exploration and creation at the *organizational, leader,* and *individual levels*. This process parallels emotional intelligence, which is rooted in self-awareness and self-management, leading to social awareness and relationship management.

Values are unique yet universal characteristics that describe how you see yourself and how you hope the world sees you. These defining traits are foundational in your behaviors, how you communicate and lead. By clearly defining values at the organizational, leader/coach, and employee levels, you more naturally develop deeper trust with others by establishing a genuine connection built upon the things that truly matter. It's important to note that shared doesn't mean the values are all the same. It indicates that they are thought about, analyzed, communicated (espoused), and enacted consistently in your daily interactions.

> A deeper understanding of the values that drive us, where they come from, and how they intersect with the world around us needs to become a curiosity movement within our relationships.

After coaching thousands of people over the years, a deeper understanding of the values that drive us, where they come from, and how they intersect with the world around us needs to become a curiosity movement within our relationships. To delve one level deeper, there are both terminal and instrumental values. Terminal values refer to end states that people desire in life (leading a prosperous life and a peaceful world). Instrumental values refer to views on acceptable models of conduct (being honest, ambitious, and ethical).

Here's a simple yet profound set of questions:

1. How do you know what may motivate someone if you don't know their values?
2. How can you fully understand someone's story if you don't understand their values?
3. How can you lead them when you don't know their values?

If I lined up your team members who are your direct reports or people you influence, could you articulate back to me their values? It's alarming that I've asked this question to thousands of leaders and their answer is usually no. This is one of the areas where we, as leader/coaches, can and must do better. It's not that we don't care; it's that we often don't take the time to determine what really drives each member of our team.

Shared values at different levels within an organization will help clearly reflect the core beliefs and principles that guide behaviors and decision-making. It has been my pleasure to collect, study, and respond to over 800 personal vision projects of my students, where they share their values and the corresponding story that supports them. This deeper understanding and curiosity changes relationships from the classroom to the boardroom.

Reflecting Vision and Values through Shared Stories

Shared stories represent the narratives and experiences that shape and reflect the culture and values at the organization, team, and individual levels. I'm a huge fan of *Ted Lasso,* and a now-famous clip from the series is a bar scene where Ted is challenged by an antagonist in the story, Rupert, to a game of darts. As Ted begins to play, he asks what he needs. He needs two triple twenties and a bull's eye. As he throws a dart, he references a quote by Walt Whitman: "Be curious, not judgmental." After he hits his first triple-double, he references that if Rupert had been more curious, he would have asked better questions like, "Have you ever played darts, Ted?" Ted would've answered with, "Yes, every Sunday afternoon in a sports bar with my father until he passed away when I was sixteen."[6] Ted then went on to hit another triple twenty and a bullseye. This is an amazing example that if we aren't curious, we don't understand someone's story and their capabilities.

> I believe that the Ted Lasso series is to coaching as Tommy Boy was to selling.

The art of story development, gathering, and telling is a core tenet of what we do within both NeuroSelling and NeuroCoaching at Braintrust. We have heard so many compelling stories through the years, and there's no doubt that it helps to align individuals, teams, and organizations with a deeper purpose, positive outcomes, and engagement.

Here's our road map for shared vision:

Shared Vision
Organizational,
Leader/Coach,
and Employee Vision & Values

Shared Vision – Organizational Level

When the organizational vision is disconnected from the leader/coach vision and the employee vision, you may observe a gap in common cause and purpose.

THE CHALLENGE: DISCONNECTED VISION

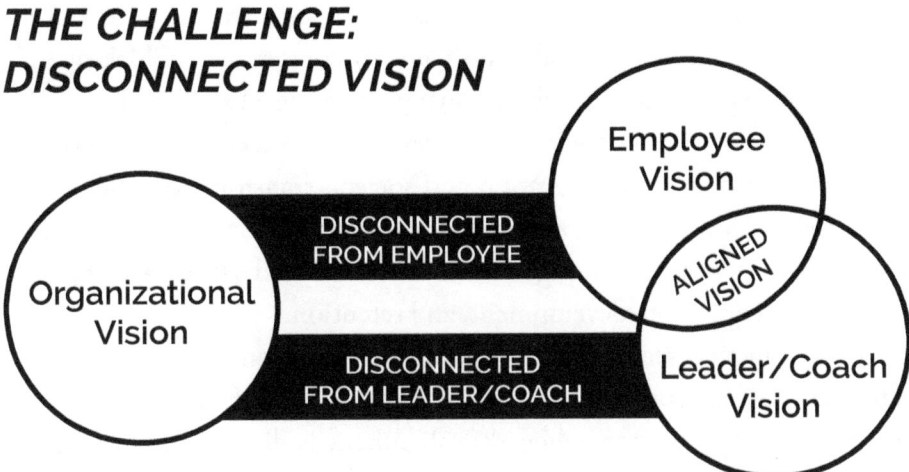

At the organizational level, shared values are the fundamental beliefs that form the foundation of the organization's culture and identity. These values are articulated in the organization's mission and vision statements. These values serve as a guiding light for the entire organization, influencing its strategies, policies, and the way in which business is conducted. Let's discuss an example that we're all familiar with—Chick-fil-A.

I'm continually amazed by the lines at any Chick-fil-A restaurant. There's no doubt that they make great chicken but also something more. When I teach undergraduates, I am often asked my opinion of this generation. I will tell you that I have great hope for the current generation because they are smart and talented. As the co-director of a leadership center at Miami University, I'm even more bullish on the future of business. The reason that I write this is based on watching the values instilled by

Chick-fil-A come to life by their employees. In the outside world, we don't have to align with these values, but I'm certain that the team members at Chick-fil-A align and thus drive a connected organizational value system. It's amazing to see the consistency from store to store and the intentional effort to carry the organizational vision forward from the drive-through to the restaurant experience. You can see it in the company's purpose—"to glorify God by being a faithful steward of all that is entrusted to us and to have a positive influence on all who come in contact with Chick-fil-A."[7] According to *QSR Magazine*, the company is nearing $19 billion in sales.[8]

We see many life sciences companies, for instance, that have robust visions centered around innovation and societal transformation yet often lack a clear vision for *people development*. It's not sufficient to merely have a statement; it must be brought to life through leadership that engages with talent acquisition, development, and retention.

In the practical realm of organizational development, the shared vision stands as a critical compass for guiding the collective efforts of a company. Yet the challenge emerges when this alignment is disrupted, particularly when the overarching organizational vision becomes disjointed from the individual visions of employees and leaders.

When an organizational vision goes off course, it's akin to the gears of a well-oiled machine grinding against each other. I'll share a brief example from an executive interview where initial values were so strong and were then challenged by growth and company ownership changes. Initially, the core values of humility, accessibility, gratitude, and advocacy resonated strongly, especially given the service that this organization provided. These values were not just words; they were the bedrock of a common purpose.

However, growth and subsequent transactions led to the erosion of these values. The impact was clear and immediate: faltering performance, slipping retention, and challenges in talent acquisition. This underlined a crucial point—the integral role of a unified organizational vision, especially one that encompasses people development as the organization went through tremendous change. In the end, the company performance—but more importantly, the culture—changed. The result was selling the company for significantly less value than was projected. Holding on to values in a VUCA (volatility, uncertainty, complexity, and ambiguity) climate is nonnegotiable.

In practice, it's essential for an organization to take a deep dive into its stated vision and values. These shouldn't just be platitudes displayed on a website; they need to be lived experiences within the company itself that are reinforced by leadership.

From a practitioner's standpoint, this approach is not just theoretical—it demands action. We need to scrutinize our corporate narratives. Is the commitment to developing people clear and unequivocal? Can our teams see and feel this commitment in their daily work?

The onus is on us as leaders to ensure that our communication is consistent, our commitment to coaching is strong, and our accountability measures are in place. We must go beyond traditional vision statements to clearly define and champion our people development vision. By doing so, we align the aspirations of our employees with the strategic direction of the organization, setting the stage for enhanced performance and a robust, people-centered culture.

At the organizational level, shared stories are the collective narratives that capture the organization's history, achievements, challenges, and pivotal moments. As leaders, we must believe and transfer stories throughout the organization. These stories are embedded as part of the organization's legacy. These stories and values connect to a broader sense of belonging, identity, and purpose. Examples of these types of stories include successes, overcoming challenges, and moments of innovation and resilience. Don't be afraid to share the positive and the negative. Think of this step as a lifeline of your organization. What are five critical moments of success and triumphs? Capture these stories and relentlessly pass them along to others, from the moments of talent acquisition to town halls and investor meetings.

> At the organizational level, shared stories are the collective narratives that capture the organization's history, achievements, challenges, and pivotal moments.

One of my dear friends, who works for Warren Buffet, once described to me that this iconic leader will host town hall meetings that last for hours. He went on to say that Warren is an amazing communicator and storyteller who'll take on any question from the organization.

Practical Coaching Tips

Coaching Tip 1: Integrate Storytelling into Your Leadership Approach

Shared stories create a powerful connection between employees and the organization's values. As a leader, make it a practice to capture and share pivotal moments—whether they are successes, challenges, or examples of resilience. Use these narratives in team meetings, onboarding sessions, and company-wide communications to reinforce your company's mission, vision, and values. Just as Chick-fil-A maintains consistency in its purpose across all locations, leaders should ensure that their teams see, hear, and feel the company's commitment to people development in their daily work. This storytelling approach helps align employees' personal aspirations with the strategic direction of the organization, fostering a culture of engagement, trust, and shared purpose.

Coaching Tip 2: Assess and Elevate Your People Development Vision

Beyond vision statements, leaders must ask: *Is our commitment to developing people clear, actionable, and continuously reinforced*? Conduct regular People Development Audits—structured reviews of how well your organization is investing in talent growth. This can include assessing leadership training, mentorship programs, career pathways, and skill development opportunities. Engage employees in this process by gathering direct feedback through surveys or focus groups. If gaps exist, take proactive steps to *create clear, visible, and measurable commitments to growth*—from structured leadership pathways to ongoing coaching and development initiatives. Organizations that consistently invest in their people not only attract top talent but also retain high performers who feel valued and see a future within the company.

Shared Vision – Leader/Coach Level

As we move into the leader/coach vision, we confront the scenario where the organizational vision and the employee vision are in harmony, but there's a disconnect with the leader/coach vision. This is what happens when your vision as a leader goes astray—you end up in "lone ranger leadership." You're riding solo, consumed by self-preservation and self-serving priorities, which inevitably leads to a path of failed execution.

Your team looks to you for consistency and leadership. They're observing, much like children do with parents, seeking stability in a chaotic world. That's why it's crucial for your leader's vision to align with the organizational and employee visions.

Let's discuss a technique to develop your leader/coach vision:

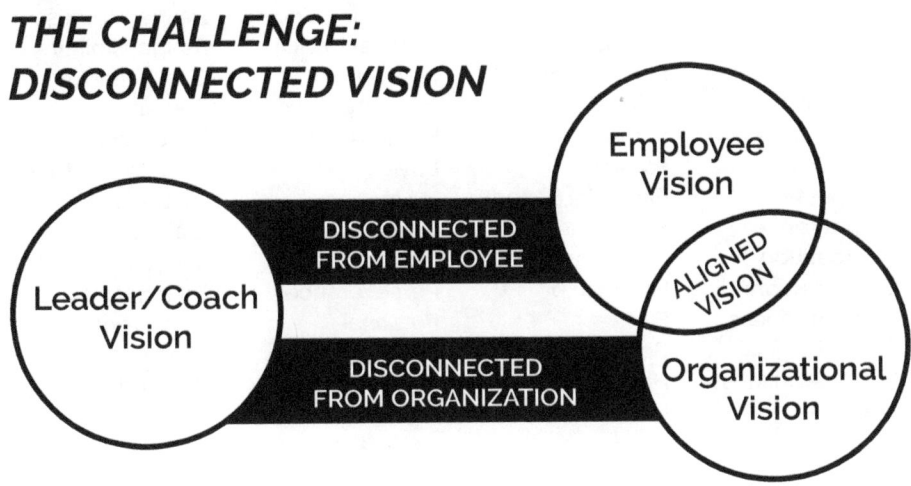

THE CHALLENGE: DISCONNECTED VISION

RESULT =
LONE RANGER LEADERSHIP, SELF-SERVING PRIORITIES, FAILED EXECUTION

It isn't enough just to list your values; you need to build them into your story. You'll use these values to live out your story while also creating a positive coaching climate where others will share their own values and stories with you. These values will inspire and motivate others on your team. If you as a leader demonstrate commitment to transparency, respect, and teamwork aligned to your values, it'll guide deeper relationships, decision-making, problem-solving, execution, and performance. So here is what we would like you to do—complete a values exercise, as identifying your top values will be a powerful reflection.

Even if you have done this exercise in the past, we encourage you to complete it again. In the exercise, you will pinpoint your top ten values, narrow them to five, and rank them. We encourage you to not overthink these. Then, critically assess how you embody where these values come from and how you enact them on a day-to-day basis.

Values

Accountability	Dedication	Health	Preparedness
Achievement	Dependability	Honesty	Pride
Adventure	Discipline	Hope	Problem-Solving
Affection	Dreamer	Humility	Recognition
Ambition	Empathy	Imagination	Reliability
Authority	Encouragement	Improving Society	Respectfulness
Autonomy	Equality	Independence	Responsibility
Coaching	Excitement	Innovation	Self-Reliance
Collaboration	Faith	Integrity	Servant
Comfortable Life	Fame	Kindess	Leadership
Companionship	Family	Love	Service to Others
Compassion	Financial Security	Mentoring	Sincerity
Competence	Forgiveness	Order	Stability
Competition	Freedom	Peace	Success
Conservation	Friendship	Perseverance	Taking Risks
Contentedness	Fun	Personal	Teamwork
Control	Genuineness	Development	Trustworthy
Courageousness	Happiness	Positivity	Winning
Creativity	Hard Work	Power	Wisdom

The next step is to think about someone who has impacted your journey. A technique I was taught is to consider three life stages (birth through eighteen, nineteen to twenty-four, and twenty-five-plus), select an impact person, and then write down the characteristics that helped you select that person. If you struggle with this, close your eyes, think of the first name that comes to your mind, and write about that person. I love this step because we realize that it's the impact of people in our lives that helps shape our stories.

> In leadership and in life, we never get to where we want to go on our own.

I'll share a bit of my story. At eighteen, I met an incredible man who later became my father-in-law and mentor. He taught me invaluable lessons in perspective and the importance of family and faith—lessons that have since been foundational to my leadership vision. We refer to my father-in-law as Chief. Chief was a two-tour helicopter pilot in Vietnam and then went on to a thirty-plus-year career at GE Aerospace.

One day, I was sitting down, talking to Chief about our corporate experiences. He said:

> "Hey, Dan, when I was in my twenties, and I was over in Vietnam, I saw life and death, and I slayed my woolly mammoth in Vietnam. So when I was sitting around the boardroom table at General Electric, I would watch people all day, every day, talk about life-and-death things in their eyes from their view. But the whole time, I was sitting there thinking that I'd seen what life and death is—and this wasn't it. I want you to learn as a foundational element to who you are—to always have perspective relative to the things that you're tackling in your personal and professional life."

Shared Vision   **81**

Then, he secondarily taught me how important faith and family are as core values and to hold onto them for all things. Chief has been there as a foundational leader for me and has shaped my leadership journey.

Now it's your turn to craft a leader vision statement. This isn't just an exercise; it's a declaration of what you stand for as a leader, meant to guide you from hiring to retirement celebrations. At our leadership center, my colleague Dr. Megan Gerhardt encourages our students (and me) to push ourselves to declare a leadership statement and then validate it with others. I had the opportunity to travel with Megan for a speaking circuit, so as I worked through my leader statement, it crystalized for me. She recommended a technique popularized by Simon Sinek. It was a statement bracketed "TO . . . SO THAT."[9]

Here's an example:

To coach with purpose and impact
so that higher-quality relationships are built.

So ponder this:

> When the people you lead reflect on their pivotal life stages and think of those who most impacted them, *will your name be on their list?*

A Moment from the Field

While working on a project with a leader from a Fortune 100 company, I once again discovered the transformative power of a shared vision. By guiding the leader through exercises focused on values and leadership influences, this seasoned executive crafted a leader vision statement, enriching his understanding of himself and his team. The leader engaged his team in similar exercises, deepening their situational conversations and fostering stronger connections. During a subsequent training, he realized the value of sharing his own story, which led to one of the most impactful sessions in his career.

This experience reinforced the critical importance of vulnerability and sharing values. The executive also highlighted the importance of understanding each team member's unique talents and strengths. As a Certified Strengths Coach, it was exciting to help them leverage strengths at all levels. By combining a shared vision with an aligned mission, you set a strong foundation for situational coaching and an enhanced coaching climate, fostering deeper development and performance. This story beautifully illustrates how essential a shared vision is in leadership and team growth.

> By combining a shared vision with an aligned mission, you set a strong foundation for situational coaching and an enhanced coaching climate, fostering deeper development and performance.

Practical Coaching Tips

Coaching Tip #1: Clarify and Align Your Leadership Vision

To avoid "lone ranger leadership," take time to assess how your personal vision aligns with both the organizational and employee vision. Reflect on your leadership values and ensure they guide your decision-making, problem-solving, and team interactions. Complete a values exercise where you identify your top ten values, narrow them to five, and critically assess how you embody them daily.

Coaching Tip #2: Reflect on Your Influential Impact People

Leadership isn't developed in isolation. Think back to three life stages (birth through eighteen, nineteen to twenty-four, and twenty-five-plus) and identify individuals who shaped your journey. Write about their impact and the characteristics that made them influential. This exercise helps reinforce the importance of relationships and mentorship in leadership, reinforcing the power of shared experiences.

Coaching Tip #3: Craft a Leadership Vision Statement

Use Simon Sinek's "TO SO THAT" framework to create a guiding statement for your leadership. This statement should encapsulate your purpose and impact as a leader. Then, validate your statement by sharing it with others and refining it based on feedback. A clear leader vision statement will serve as your guiding principle, ensuring consistency in your leadership approach.

By applying these steps, leaders can bridge the gap between their vision and the organization's and foster deeper connections with their teams.

Shared Vision – Employee Level

Tackling the employee vision is where the rubber meets the road in leadership. It's about understanding the unique makeup of every individual on your team. As the well-known leader-member exchange theory teaches us, it is difficult to coach without understanding the unique makeup of every individual on your team. Coaching isn't a one-size-fits-all deal; it's personal, and let's be real—it's tough. If you're going to help team members chart a course to their goals and drive performance, you need to roll up your sleeves and dive into their stories.

> If you're going to help team members chart a course to their goals and drive performance, you need to roll up your sleeves and dive into their stories.

Get those values. And don't just collect them—really dig into their origins. Listen to the stories behind them. You can utilize the same process for your employees to obtain their values and stories. And don't stop there. What strengths do they bring to the table? (We will discuss this more in the next section.) There might be hidden talents you're not even aware of because you haven't asked. Play to your team members' strengths—that's where the magic happens. Values, strengths, and dreams will help you better understand each team member's journey to this point and how you can help put them on a path to subsequent chapters. I'm talking about their vision of fulfillment, both personal and professional. Be their champion and help them get there. When you align with their values and vision, you unlock something special. Employees demonstrating shared values might show a commitment to quality, a collaborative spirit, and a positive work ethic.

Shared stories are the experiences and narratives that individuals and teams share about their work, challenges, successes, and everyday life in the organization. These stories, similar to the other levels of shared vision, will build cohesion and knowledge and foster a deeper sense of community within the team. Stories are powerful, and they not only positively modulate neurochemistry but they also build deeper connections and relationships.

So ultimately, every team member's story matters.

Practical Coaching Tips

Coaching Tip #1: Host Values-Discovery Conversations

Instead of assuming what drives your employees, set up intentional one-on-one conversations where they can share their personal and professional values. Ask open-ended questions like:

- "What experiences have shaped the way you approach work?"
- "What aspects of your job make you feel most fulfilled?"
- "If you could design your ideal work environment, what would it look like?"

The key is to actively listen and dig deeper into the origins of these values. Understanding the "why" behind their priorities will allow you to align their work with what truly matters to them.

Coaching Tip #2: Create a Strengths-Based Action Plan

After uncovering an employee's values and strengths, take action by co-developing a personalized growth plan. This could include:

- Assigning projects that align with their strengths and career aspirations
- Encouraging them to mentor others in areas they excel
- Providing opportunities for professional development based on their vision of success

By playing to their strengths and aligning their work with their personal vision, you not only boost engagement but also create a more motivated and purpose-driven team.

The magic happens when the organization's vision aligns seamlessly with both the leader's vision and the personal visions of team members. When this alignment occurs, teams move beyond functioning to truly thriving. However, achieving this level of synergy is no small feat.

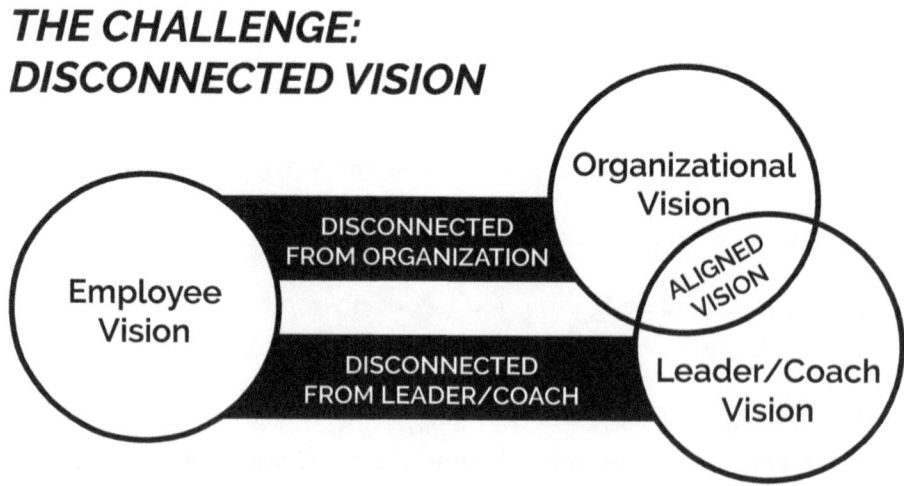

The encouraging news is that tools exist to help you embed these strategies into your leadership practice. Even if the only takeaway from this book is a commitment to fostering a people-centered vision, you will already be on a transformative path.

As we finish up at basecamp of shared vision in this chapter and prepare for the ascent to aligned mission in the next, it's important to remember that a clear vision for people development, combined with an authentic and vulnerable leadership approach, is the formula for impactful coaching.

Top NeuroCoaching Takeaways

1. **Shared vision is the foundation of meaningful leadership.**

   This isn't just about strategy; it's about aligning values, vision, strategy, standards, and strengths at the organizational, leader, and individual levels. A *shared vision* aligns an organization's mission with the daily actions of its people, fostering trust, motivation, and high-impact collaboration.

2. **The three pillars of NeuroCoaching drive transformation.**

   Shared vision, situational conversations, and the coaching climate are all key elements to the NeuroCoaching playbook that lead to reduced turnover, as shown with the life science company case study.

3. **Values and strengths-based leadership create meaningful connections.**

   Leaders should define and articulate their *core values*, reflect on their *mentors*, and *craft* a leadership vision statement using Simon Sinek's "TO SO THAT" framework in order to prevent "lone ranger leadership."

4. **Coaching is personal.**

   Leaders need to understand and align with their employees' visions. Coaching isn't one-size-fits-all; it requires understanding employees' personal values, strengths, and career aspirations.

CHAPTER 7

ALIGNED MISSION

> *Perfection is not attainable, but if we chase perfection, we can catch excellence.*
> —Vince Lombardi

THROUGHOUT THE LAST chapter, our goal has been to equip you with a journey map for assessing shared vision at multiple levels—organization, leader, and team member. The second part of the formula we refer to as the 3S's—*strategy with execution, standards with accountability,* and *strengths with skills*—allows us to further build out a road map for operational and transactional excellence. As we leave the base camp of shared vision—where we've aligned on vision and values—it's time to begin the next critical ascent: mastering the power of *aligned mission*.

If shared vision is the foundation that keeps us tethered to purpose, aligned mission is the next elevation that determines whether we move with focus, unity, accountability, and impact. Can you imagine climbing a mountain without establishing clear standards in the lower-risk parts of the journey? Or setting off without knowing the expectations—or how you'll hold each other accountable? What about failing to identify the unique strengths and essential skills each climber brings to the team?

When we first built this framework, we underestimated how vital these "3 S's"—strategy, standards, and strengths—would be to the climb. That changed last year. During multiple workshops, leaders challenged us to not just teach these elements but to help them bring them to life inside their shared vision. So that's what we did—and it shifted everything.

As we ascend to the next level, it's important to remember what the best climbers know: Acclimatization matters. Progress isn't always a straight path—sometimes, you have to move back and forth to adjust to the new altitude. If you're ready to elevate yourself and the team to reach the next camp, let's take that next step together.

Strategy with Execution: Approach to Strategic Alignment

Imagine stepping into the NFL Hall of Fame, surrounded by legends who achieved greatness through teamwork, a unified vision, and an aligned mission. It doesn't matter whether you're in a room with NFL legends, sitting with an emerging cyber security firm, climbing a mountain, or producing a Broadway show—success in all these different environments requires an aligned mission that includes strategy, standards, and strengths. It was one of my mentors who, after a decade in marketing as an amazing leader/coach, reinforced with us the power of having a *process* for creating a set of the 3S's. I could have never imagined at that time that it would find its way into your hands.

Mastering the power of an aligned mission starts with implementing the first S in the 3S's—*strategy with execution*. As I sat this year with an emerging cybersecurity company in Austin, Texas, we were able to build a road map for their next two-year to three-year journey. As in any good adventure, we took a structured approach to their strategy. We started with defining key words like vision, values, mission, and the word of the year to capture the DNA of the company. From there, we identified critical market segments and articulated the strategic imperatives required to grow in each one. We then outlined the tactical support needed for each strategy, clarified the standards of excellence that would guide execution, documented key performance indicators, and created a tight link to both their short-term goals and their long-term desired future state. This process is a nonnegotiable part of a substantiated and aligned mission, much like the gear, planning, and discipline required to summit any mountain worth climbing. Without it, a team may start strong, but they risk veering off course, underestimating terrain, or running out of resources before reaching the peak. Just as seasoned climbers carefully map their route, train for the conditions, and define their checkpoints along the way, organizations must align strategy with execution, knowing exactly where they're headed and how they'll measure progress as they ascend.

Vision: The Foundation of Strategic Alignment

As discussed in Chapter 6, every organization needs a clearly articulated vision that serves as a guiding light. This vision should inspire and unite leaders, teams, and individuals toward a common goal. In the NeuroCoaching framework, vision is not just a statement; it's a unifying force that drives decision-making, engagement, and growth.

Values: The Cornerstone of Organizational Behavior

As we have discussed, values define how an organization behaves, both internally and externally. They set expectations for interactions, ethical decision-making, and cultural cohesion. When values are clearly documented and embraced, they serve as an internal compass for leaders and teams, reinforcing accountability and commitment to strategic goals.

Mission: The Execution of Purpose

A mission statement defines why an organization exists and how it differentiates itself in the marketplace. It's the practical execution of the vision, aligning employees and stakeholders to a shared purpose. In small, midsize, and enterprise businesses, aligning mission with daily operations ensures focus, consistency, and measurable impact.

The Word of the Year: One Focused Theme for Impact

To unify efforts, organizations should define *one word* that encapsulates their core focus for the year. This word serves as a rallying point for leaders and teams, reinforcing commitment to the overarching strategy. Examples include:

- Momentum: Driving continuous progress and sustained growth
- Resilience: Strengthening adaptability in a changing market
- Excellence: Committing to high standards in execution and results
- Agility: Embracing flexibility and innovation
- Collaboration: Enhancing cross-functional teamwork and partnerships

Top Three Adjectives to Describe the Organization

Descriptive adjectives help reinforce the organization's brand identity and cultural DNA. Examples include:

- Innovative: Emphasizing forward-thinking solutions and continuous improvement
- Customer-Centric: Placing the client experience at the heart of every initiative
- High-Performing: Committed to excellence, efficiency, and measurable results

Identified Market Segments for Targeted Growth

Clearly defining *market segments* ensures that all strategies align with customer needs and business opportunities. Examples of segmentation include:

- Enterprise Clients: Large organizations requiring tailored solutions
- Mid-Market Companies: Growth-oriented firms needing scalable services
- Small Businesses: Emerging companies seeking agile and affordable options
- Healthcare & Life Sciences: Companies with specialized compliance and innovation needs
- Technology & SaaS (Software as a Service): Businesses focused on digital transformation and automation

Strategic Imperatives: The Core Priorities

A successful organization establishes three to five strategic imperatives that serve as the primary focus for the year. These imperatives drive high-impact results and ensure that every department and team is moving toward common objectives. Examples of strategic imperatives include:

- Market Expansion – Entering new markets or expanding within existing ones
- Operational Excellence – Improving efficiency, reducing costs, and streamlining processes
- Customer Experience Enhancement – Elevating service quality, engagement, and satisfaction

- Innovation Leadership – Advancing product development, technology, or service offerings
- Talent Development – Strengthening leadership, coaching, and workforce capabilities

Tactical Support for Each Strategy

For each strategic imperative, tactical plans define the execution steps required for success. Tactical support involves identifying *specific actions* that align with strategy. For example:

- Market Expansion: Launch a regional marketing campaign, identify strategic partnerships, and enhance lead generation efforts
- Operational Excellence: Implement process automation, optimize supply chain logistics, and improve cross-functional collaboration
- Customer Experience Enhancement: Deploy AI-driven customer service solutions, implement proactive outreach, and refine onboarding processes
- Innovation Leadership: Establish an R&D task force, launch pilot programs, and leverage customer feedback loops
- Talent Development: Implement leadership training, expand mentorship programs, and enhance performance management systems

Standards of Excellence Under Each Tactical Plan

Every tactical plan should be executed under *defined standards of excellence* to ensure consistency and accountability. These standards include:

- Quality Benchmarks: Measurable criteria to assess the effectiveness of execution

- Performance Metrics: Quantifiable standards for evaluating individual and team contributions

- Cultural Alignment: Ensuring every initiative reflects organizational values and leadership expectations

- Continuous Improvement: Ongoing assessment, refinement, and optimization of strategies

Documented KPIs to Measure Success

Key Performance Indicators (KPIs) serve as quantifiable measurements of success. Effective KPIs should be *specific, measurable, achievable, relevant,* and *time-bound* (SMART). Examples of KPIs linked to strategic imperatives:

- Market Expansion: Increase regional revenue by 15 percent year over year.

- Operational Excellence: Reduce operational costs by 10 percent within six months.

- Customer Experience Enhancement: Improve Net Promoter Score (NPS) from 75 to 85.

- Innovation Leadership: Launch two new product features within the fiscal year.

- Talent Development: Increase employee engagement scores by 20 percent.

Linking Strategy to a Desired Future State (Goals)

The ultimate goal of this structured approach is to align strategy with a desired future state, ensuring financial performance is directly connected to operational excellence. This road map helps businesses transition from strategic planning to execution with accountability by doing the following:

- Documenting alignment between mission, strategy, and execution.
- Ensuring financial growth is measured through clear KPIs.
- Creating a leadership culture that sustains engagement and accountability.
- Building a scalable model for continuous improvement.

Practical Coaching Tips

Coaching Tip #1: Implementing a Strategy Map

Organizations should document their strategic alignment using a *one-page strategy map* that includes:

- Vision, mission, and values.
- Strategic imperatives (three to five key priorities for the year).
- Tactical support plans under each strategy.
- Standards of excellence for execution.
- Documented KPIs for measurable success.
- Market segments for targeted growth.
- The selected *word of the year* and the *top three adjectives* to reinforce the organizational identity.

Coaching Tip #2: Quarterly Strategic Review Process

A quarterly review ensures strategic alignment remains dynamic and adaptable. This process should involve:

1. Reviewing KPIs: Assessing performance data and identifying gaps.

2. Evaluating Market Changes: Adjusting strategies based on shifts in customer needs or industry trends.

3. Reinforcing the Word of the Year: Ensuring the chosen theme remains a priority in decision-making.

4. Leadership Coaching Sessions: Using the NeuroCoaching approach to enhance leader impact.

5. Adjusting Tactical Execution: Refining action plans to optimize results.

By following this structured approach to strategy with execution, organizations can create a unified, high-performing, and strategically aligned culture that drives sustained success. This focus on strategy with execution within the framework of an aligned mission ensures that every leader and team member will have a consistent journey map for short- and long-term impact, ensuring operations with clarity, purpose, and measurable progress. Let's move forward to the second of the 3S's—the power of shared standards with accountability.

Standards with Accountability: The Glue That Binds Teams

At every level of an organization, shared standards establish cohesion and clarity. Organizational standards provide direction, leaders embody and reinforce these principles, and employees incorporate them into daily behaviors. When effectively implemented, shared standards function as the social glue that holds a team together.

Cohesion is often described as the degree of camaraderie and unity within a team or group. Think back to a time when you were a part of a highly cohesive group—perhaps a sports team, a high-performing work environment, or even a close-knit family. There was likely an unspoken understanding of expectations, responsibilities, and shared values. That's the power of shared standards—they create an environment where individuals feel connected, accountable, and aligned toward a common goal.

A personal experience that highlights the importance of shared standards took place last summer when my friend Dave and I embarked on a long-anticipated motorcycle trip to Colorado (not quite Mt. Everest). Months of planning had gone into the journey, and on the morning of departure, we met at a Dunkin' Donuts, packed our last pieces of gear, and set off.

> That's the power of shared standards—they create an environment where individuals feel connected, accountable, and aligned toward a common goal.

From the outset, shared standards dictated the structure of our trip. We had clear expectations regarding driving shifts—every three hours, we alternated. We established a budget strategy, taking turns paying for gas. We agreed on the types of stops we would make, from dining choices to lodging decisions—hotel versus tent. These predefined standards facilitated seamless communication, minimized misunderstandings, and ensured a positive experience.

Of course, not everything went according to plan. There were unexpected detours and challenges, but because we had a framework for decision-making, we adapted with ease. The shared standards gave us clarity, allowing us to pivot without losing sight of our ultimate goal.

The same principle applies to building a shared vision within an organization. Establishing clear, well-communicated standards enables leaders and teams to move forward cohesively, ensuring accountability and alignment.

Legendary basketball coach Mike Krzyzewski (Coach K), a five-time national champion and three-time Olympic gold medalist, articulates this concept well in his book *The Gold Standard*:

Standards are lived. This is what we do all the time... These are the things for which we hold one another accountable. Once a group of individuals formulates and agrees to their standards, they become united, single-minded in purpose... Standards should never go unspoken.[1]

Establishing and Upholding Shared Standards

Through our work with leaders across industries, we've found that implementing shared standards requires a deliberate process. It begins with identifying the categories of excellence critical to your team's success. Once these categories are established, defining nonnegotiable standards of excellence provides clarity. From there, aligning key performance indicators (KPIs) with standards and connecting them to overarching goals ensures a structured approach to accountability.

To illustrate, let's consider the role of a production team leader for a Broadway show:

Function: production leadership team.

Categories of Excellence: Casting, tech planning, rehearsal excellence, performance excellence, and company culture.

Category Focus: Rehearsal excellence.

Standard of Excellence: Rehearsals start and end on time. Actors are ready five minutes ahead of rehearsal, and the production team reserves the last five minutes for cast questions and next steps.

KPI: The stage manager tracks rehearsal times in a shared Google Drive document, reviewed every Monday at 5:00 p.m.

Goal: Rehearsal discipline leads to 100 percent readiness for tech week.

This example demonstrates the structured approach needed to ensure alignment and accountability. Whether applied to a Broadway production, a corporate sales or operations team, or even a family unit, shared standards create the necessary structure for high performance.

At the organizational level, shared standards define the guiding principles embedded within a company's mission, vision, and core values. This applies not just at a corporate level but within functional areas such as sales, customer service, or operations. High-performing organizations establish a seamless connection between overarching organizational standards and the specific roles that departments play in achieving strategic goals.

As one of my mentors once told me, "If you don't have a clear set of standards, you can't define a plan to move from where you are to where you want to be." The best organizations recognize this truth, ensuring that strategic imperatives, tactical execution, and resource allocation align with their current stage of growth.

At the leader/coach level, shared standards manifest in the behaviors and expectations modeled by leadership. As a leader, your responsibility is to bridge the gap between organizational directives and day-to-day execution within your team. This includes establishing clarity around procedures, communication expectations, performance benchmarks, and cross-functional collaboration.

For team members, shared standards shape the norms and behaviors that govern daily work. Employees crave consistency and clear expectations, as these factors contribute to a stable, high-performance environment. Elements such as role clarity, communication protocols, and professional conduct guidelines fall within this domain.

Practical Coaching Tips

Coaching Tip #1: Create a Shared Standards Exercise

Gather your team and identify the categories of excellence that define success in your specific environment. Define the nonnegotiable standards for each category and align them with measurable KPIs and goals. Whether it's within a business unit, a creative project, or a personal endeavor, this exercise provides clarity and fosters alignment.

Coaching Tip #2: Make Standards Visible and Actionable

A standard is only effective if it is consistently reinforced. Establish routines—whether through team check-ins, accountability reviews, or performance dashboards—to ensure that shared standards remain a living, breathing aspect of your culture.

Without shared standards, teams operate in ambiguity, making accountability a challenge. But when expectations are clearly defined and reinforced, teams not only perform better—they thrive. The key is to create a framework that provides structure without stifling adaptability, ensuring your organization remains resilient and future focused.

Strengths with Skills: Unlocking Your Talents

Over thirty million people worldwide have taken an assessment to uncover their unique strengths, and for good reason. Understanding our strengths—what we often refer to as talents—provides a road map to optimizing performance, deepening engagement, and achieving operational excellence.

In NeuroCoaching, we believe that unlocking and intentionally leveraging these talents is essential for leaders, teams, and organizations. Talents are naturally recurring patterns of thought, feeling, or behavior that can be productively applied. When these raw talents are identified and cultivated with the right skills and strategies, they become powerful assets, propelling individuals and teams toward excellence.

According to Gallup's extensive research, people who focus on their strengths are three times more likely to report having an excellent quality of life. They are also six times more likely to be engaged in their work.[2] Engagement, in this context, is not merely about motivation or job satisfaction; it is about being deeply connected to one's role, operating in a flow state where natural talents are aligned with meaningful work.

As a Gallup Certified Strengths Coach, I have witnessed firsthand the transformation that occurs when individuals understand, verbalize, and optimize their strengths. Conversations gain depth, performance elevates, and engagement skyrockets. Yet the true power of strengths is not just in recognizing them—it is in investing in them. Simply knowing your strengths is not enough. Without active cultivation, they remain untapped potential rather than a driving force for excellence.

My Strengths Journey: Awareness, Activation, and Application

As a leader, I have taken a close look at how my top five strengths—Achiever, Communication, Positivity, WOO (Winning Others Over), and Maximizer—shape my operational excellence.

Achiever pushes me to set high standards, constantly seeking the next milestone. While this fuels productivity, it can also lead to burnout if not balanced with strategic rest and delegation. Communication allows me to articulate ideas with clarity and passion, a vital skill in both coaching and leadership. However, unchecked, it can lead to talking more than listening. Positivity brings energy and enthusiasm to my interactions, but it also requires awareness to ensure it does not downplay real challenges that need addressing. WOO helps build relationships effortlessly, yet it demands discipline to ensure that deep, meaningful connections are prioritized over surface-level rapport. Lastly, Maximizer drives me to refine and elevate everything I do, but without boundaries, it can lead to perfectionism that stifles progress.

> A crucial part of NeuroCoaching is teaching individuals and teams how to channel their strengths effectively, leveraging their talents while mitigating the risks that come with them.

This awareness has helped me not only harness my strengths but also recognize their potential pitfalls. Strengths can become blind spots if not intentionally aimed. A crucial part of NeuroCoaching is teaching individuals and teams how to channel their strengths effectively, leveraging their talents while mitigating the risks that come with them.

Strengths in Action: Building High-Performing Teams

A strengths-based team is not a team of perfect individuals. Instead, it is a group of talented contributors, each bringing unique capabilities to the table, valued for their strengths and aware of their interdependencies.

In one organization I worked with, a leadership team was struggling with engagement and turnover. After conducting a strengths assessment, we uncovered a striking pattern: The team was heavily weighted in strategic and execution strengths but lacked representation in relationship-building talents. The team excelled in planning and achieving results but struggled with fostering trust, collaboration, and psychological safety.

Once these insights were revealed, we designed a coaching strategy that helped leaders not only acknowledge the gaps but actively invest in relationship-building behaviors. Some leaders intentionally partnered with colleagues whose strengths complemented their own, while others made simple yet impactful changes, such as dedicating more time to one-on-one conversations with team members. The result? Improved communication, greater cohesion, and a noticeable increase in engagement. The organization saw a reduction in turnover and a measurable boost in productivity.

Practical Coaching Tips

Coaching Tip #1: Discover Your Strengths

If you have never taken a strengths assessment, the first step is to work with a Gallup-certified coach (or reach out to us) to uncover your top talents. Understanding these strengths is the foundation for meaningful personal and professional development.

Coaching Tip #2: Apply the "Name, Claim, and Aim" Framework

- *Name your strengths* – Identify your natural talents and recognize how they show up in your daily work.

- *Claim them* – Take ownership of your strengths, understanding how they contribute to your success.

- *Aim them toward excellence* – Actively invest in your strengths, refining and applying them in ways that elevate performance and engagement.

Coaching Tip #3: Build a Strengths-Based Strategy

If you already know your strengths, revisit them. Are you actively using them? Dust them off and develop a plan to integrate them into your daily leadership and work habits. Design specific ways to communicate and incorporate your strengths in interactions with colleagues, clients, and team members.

Coaching Tip #4: Understand the Full Spectrum

Gallup's assessment identifies thirty-four strengths, and while your top five are critical, unlocking the full spectrum can provide deeper self-awareness and insight into areas for growth.

Strengths: A Catalyst for Performance and Purpose

The essence of strengths-based coaching is not just about identifying what we do well but intentionally developing and applying those talents in ways that create impact. NeuroCoaching harnesses this approach to drive transformation at the individual, team, and organizational levels.

By understanding and leveraging our strengths, we don't just improve performance—we build engagement, foster operational excellence, and cultivate a work environment where individuals thrive. Strengths are more than labels; they are tools for creating momentum, connection, and lasting success.

> By understanding and leveraging our strengths, we don't just improve performance—we build engagement, foster operational excellence, and cultivate a work environment where individuals thrive.

The question isn't whether you have strengths—the question is, are you using them to their full potential? Now is the time to unlock them, refine them, and aim them toward your greatest impact.

In this part of the book, we've explored the concept of a shared vision at multiple levels and an aligned mission through strategy, standards, and strengths. We've laid the groundwork for creating a cohesive and aligned team. With that in place, we can now recenter back on our definition of coaching and shift our attention to *situational conversations,* the next crucial component of the NeuroCoaching framework.

Coaching is a communication skill that drives sustained growth and performance through tailored situational conversations, and these intentional dialogues will empower us as leaders to effectively navigate decision-making and foster meaningful engagement within our teams.

Going back to our mountain climbing analogy, these situational conversations are akin to running the ridgelines of communication excellence—those high-stakes, high-impact moments where leaders guide others with clarity and intention. Just like navigating a mountain ridge requires awareness, adaptability, and precision, coaching demands presence and skill at each critical juncture.

Along this path, leaders encounter six key ridgeline intersections: purpose, perspective, plan/path, progress, problems, and performance. These are the pivotal moments where a well-timed conversation can change the course of a relationship, a team, or even an entire organization. Each intersection presents an opportunity to build trust, align vision, and elevate outcomes. Mastering these tailored conversations equips leaders to scale the peaks of growth and impact—one intentional step at a time.

Top NeuroCoaching Takeaways

1. **A shared vision requires strategic alignment.**

    Organizations that clearly define *strategic imperatives* (such as market expansion, operational excellence, and talent development) can align their teams toward meaningful and measurable outcomes.

2. **Leveraging strengths unlocks performance and engagement.**

    Understanding an individual's and team's *strengths* (talents) is crucial for optimizing performance and fostering engagement.

3. **Strategic execution requires ongoing review and adaptation.**

    To ensure success, leaders should implement a quarterly strategic review process that assesses standards, KPIs, and goals to refine tactical execution.

CHAPTER 8

SITUATIONAL CONVERSATIONS

The single biggest problem in communication is the illusion that it has taken place.
—George Bernard Shaw

HAVE YOU EVER heard of a *green-light meeting* in Hollywood? If not, let me paint a picture for you—one that goes far beyond the film industry and straight into the heart of leadership, coaching, and the defining moments that shape our paths.

A green-light meeting is the pivotal moment when a movie's fate is decided. Studio executives, producers, and creative leads gather to assess every aspect of a film—its script, budget, cast, and marketing strategy. If given the green light, the film moves forward into production. If not, it might be reworked, delayed, or scrapped entirely. But some green-light meetings transcend business as usual. And there's no better example than the now-famous *Greatest Showman* meeting—one that almost didn't happen.

Hugh Jackman, the star of the film, had just undergone surgery to remove skin cancer from his nose. He was under strict doctor's orders *not* to sing. But this was the moment. The dream of *The Greatest Showman* teetered on the edge, and the meeting's outcome would determine if the project moved forward or collapsed entirely.

Jackman showed up anyway. Not just physically, but *fully*. At first, he tried to hold back, honoring the medical restrictions. But as the music swelled and the energy in the room ignited, he couldn't help himself. He sang. And not just sang—he *poured* himself into the performance. The passion in his voice, the raw emotion on his face, the connection between him and the other performers—everything about that moment was contagious. By the time the song ended, the decision was made. The room was electric. The film was greenlit.

Why? Because emotional contagion is *real*. When someone brings their full passion and conviction to a moment, others feel it too.

This is what great coaching conversations should feel like.

Every time you sit down with a team member, you have the opportunity to create a *green-light moment*—a situational moment of impact that shapes their confidence, their choices, and their future. Does your coaching conversation send them forward with a *green light*—energized, confident, and ready to act? Or do they walk away with a *yellow light*—hesitant, uncertain? Worse yet, does it feel like a *red light* where doubt and frustration take hold?

Great coaching isn't about just giving advice. It's about creating an environment where trust and truth fuel action. It's about inspiring people to *believe*—just like Jackman did in that room, just like *The Greatest Showman* did for audiences around the world. So the next time you sit across from a team member, ask yourself: *Am I creating a green-light moment?* Because when you do—it's not just a conversation. It's a moment that could change everything.

In the journey of leadership, every decision point is a moment of impact—much like navigating through a city full of stoplights. At these intersections, there are six critical components to consider, which comprise the communication framework known as the 6P's. The 6P's are purpose, perspective, plan/path, progress, problems, and performance, and they are designed to improve our situational conversation skills to allow enhanced situational fluency (intentional movement) within our conversations.

Trust is the foundation of all effective communication. Without personal connection and professional credibility, we risk running through a red light, jeopardizing trust.

Stoplight 1: Purpose – Understanding the purpose of each conversation is crucial. When we align on the "why," it transforms interactions, preserves time, and fosters deeper engagement.

Stoplight 2: Perspective – By considering others' viewpoints, we downregulate emotions and build self-awareness, which is essential for effective communication.

Stoplight 3: Plan/Path – A well-defined plan helps keep us on track. It serves as a road map, allowing us to measure progress effectively.

Stoplight 4: Progress – Co-generating progress with team members is key. When they seek our guidance on their development, it strengthens the coaching relationship.

Stoplight 5: Problems – Addressing barriers proactively reduces risks and maintains performance.

Stoplight 6: Performance – The consistent delivery of meaningful results driven by clarity, commitment, and measurable growth.

> *"Every coaching conversation is a situational moment of impact that generates from a place of trust and truth."*

The Journey of Transformation: A NeuroCoaching Perspective

When Matt first approached me with the idea of running the 1999 inaugural Flying Pig Marathon in Cincinnati, Ohio, I thought he was joking. I had never even run a 5K, let alone a full marathon. If we had only focused on the daunting 26.2 miles ahead, the goal would have seemed impossible—too overwhelming to even begin. Instead, we set out on a journey that would redefine our limits, deepen our friendship, and prove the power of a *shared vision, shared mission,* and *situational coaching.*

Shared Vision: Aligning Purpose and Possibility

Matt and I had been friends for nearly a decade. We spoke often, spent time with our families, and our spouses—though skeptical of our sanity—fully supported the idea of running a marathon. We were both busy professionals: Matt was an entrepreneur navigating the demands of a new business, and I worked for a Fortune 100 healthcare company with frequent travel.

Our shared vision started as *let's run a marathon* but evolved into *let's push ourselves beyond what we believe is possible.* This wasn't just about running; it was about *commitment, resilience,* and *achieving something together that neither of us could do alone.*

Aligned Mission: Turning Commitment into Action

Understanding that success wouldn't come from just good intentions, we set clear standards:

- 5:30 a.m. training sessions when we weren't traveling.
- Independent training on the road with regular check-ins.
- Weekend long runs together for accountability.

We knew that consistency and discipline were key, not just for physical endurance but for mental toughness.

Shared Values: The Fuel That Kept Us Going

Adventure had always been at the core of our friendship. We had already tackled a seventy-five-mile kayak trip on the Ohio River, and we thrived on testing our limits. Beyond adventure, we shared core values of *family, dedication, determination,* and *perseverance*—all of which would be tested in the months ahead.

Situational Conversations: Coaching through the Crossroads

The training began in the dead of winter. A dark, frigid January morning awaited us for our first run. Snow flurries danced in our headlamp beams as we met on the bike trail. It was below freezing.

That morning, the excitement of the goal was gone—replaced by fear. I felt the weight of doubt settling in:

- *What if I can't do it?*
- *What if I get hurt?*
- *What if I have the wrong gear?*
- *What if I get sick?*

We all experience these moments—the ones where excitement meets reality, and fear threatens to keep us from taking the first step. The overwhelming nature of the goal can lead to paralysis, making us retreat into what feels safe.

But this is where *situational conversations* made all the difference.

Matt recognized that, in this moment, I needed perspective, not just motivation. Instead of focusing on the *entire* race, he redirected my attention to *just the next step.*

> *"Let's focus on today. Just this run.
> That's all that matters right now."*

His approach reflected *the six key decision intersections in coaching*:

- **Purpose** – He reminded me why we started: adventure, challenge, and growth.

- **Perspective** – Instead of the whole marathon, he helped me focus on *this* run.

- **Plan/Path** – He didn't overwhelm me with strategy; he just told me to take the next step.

- **Problems** – He assured me setbacks were normal (including some foot pain), and we consistently measured the plan, path, and progress.

- **Progress** – We measured our progress on a daily basis with constant communication through the ups and downs of a long journey.

- **Performance** – As we continued on the journey to race day, we never stopped assessing our performance on a daily, weekly, and monthly basis. Every step of the way, we connected it back to our vision and mission.

This is the power of *situational coaching conversations*—guiding someone through their crossroads, one decision at a time.

Transformation: When Goals Evolve

As training continued, something unexpected happened. At first, our goal was simply to *finish* the marathon. But as we built confidence, the vision evolved. We started to believe in something bigger: *breaking the four-hour mark*. The journey wasn't just about crossing a finish line—it was about realizing *what we were truly capable of*.

When race day arrived, we stood side-by-side at the starting line, ready. Every early morning, every setback, every coaching conversation had led us here. And when we finally crossed the finish line—*in under four hours*—we had not only achieved our goal but redefined our own limits.

The NeuroCoaching Takeaway

This journey was more than just running a marathon—it was a living example of how NeuroCoaching transforms *mindset, performance,* and *relationships*:

Shared Vision kept us committed through doubt.

Aligned Mission turned ideas into consistent operational excellence and action.

Situational Conversations guided us through moments of hesitation and fear.

Great leaders, like great coaches, help others see *what's possible beyond their own doubts.* Whether you're coaching a team member, leading an organization, or pushing yourself toward a personal goal, the same principles apply:

Meet people where they are, help them take the next step, and watch their vision expand beyond what they ever believed possible.

Just like training for a marathon, navigating leadership and coaching conversations requires more than just a rigid plan—it demands adaptability, awareness, and the ability to meet people where they are. Throughout our journey to the finish line, the most pivotal moments weren't in the structured training schedule but in the *situational conversations*—the moments of doubt, motivation, recalibration, and breakthrough.

In leadership, coaching, and even high-stakes business environments, success isn't just about having a strategy; it's about *situational fluency*—the ability to recognize where someone is in their journey and guide them through the critical intersections of decision-making. This is where the Six P's of NeuroCoaching come back into play:

- *Trust* – Establishing a foundation for open, meaningful dialogue.

- *Purpose* – Aligning the conversation to something meaningful and motivating.

- *Perspective* – Seeing the challenge through their eyes before offering solutions.

- *Plan/Path* – Co-creating the next steps with clarity and confidence.

- *Progress* – Measuring progress daily.

- *Problems* – Proactively addressing barriers.

- *Performance* – Driving sustained success through ongoing coaching and reinforcement.

To coach effectively and inspire meaningful change, we must become fluent in these situational conversations—understanding when to push, when to listen, when to strategize, and when to adjust.

At the outset, the 6P framework may appear to be a rigid step-by-step approach to communication that wouldn't allow for situational fluency. In fact, this is furthest from the truth. Learning a process so you can become consciously competent in what you are doing allows you to be *more* situationally fluent within a conversation. Let's define situational conversations and situational fluency.

Imagine stepping into your next coaching conversation, full of confidence—able to navigate different contexts and circumstances seamlessly. Think about your level of situational fluency. But are you really adapting to each moment, or just hoping for the best?

A 2023 article in *Fortune* stated, "Thanks to AI, workers are struggling with FOBO (fear of being obsolete). As soon as this year or next, AI *fluency* will become more inarguable for workers to stay competitive in the job market."[1] I found this fascinating on two fronts. First, the concept of

FOBO fascinated me because I historically only considered FOMO (fear of missing out). Second, it's the point that we're talking about AI fluency, but the paradox is that we still aren't actively engaging in situational fluency within our own communication. There's no doubt that AI is rapidly changing the world around us. But with that in mind, here's what we also know and must engage in—even with all this technology and information at our fingertips, we, as leader/coaches, remain at the heart of guiding our teams. Communication is still the foundation of leadership. If we fail to develop situational fluency, we may encounter both FOBO and FOMO!

As Dr. Ken Blanchard (creator of the Situational Leadership II® model) says, "The new generation of workers demand a partnership model where leadership is more about influence, dialogue, and collaboration. Leaders will be challenged with creating engaging work environments where they inspire people to bring their best creativity to work."[2]

Conversational and Situational Fluency

Effective communicators can change or adapt their styles to fit the situational context and move appropriately along a spectrum of relational versus transactional orientation. I would like you to think about this as a balance or dosing of how we evaluate a situation, consider the task, understand the relationship, and fluidly move through the conversation. One of my favorite *Harvard Business Review* articles, "Why Highly Efficient Leaders Fail," states that "the high levels of efficiency that allow highly task-focused leaders to be so productive often come at the expense of a more people-based focus."[3]

In the book *Scaling Leadership*, Robert Anderson and William Adams discuss that great leaders foster deep relationships and that the deeper the relationships, the more solid the foundations and, therefore, power in being radically human—including vulnerability with unusual degrees of humility, self-awareness, courage, and integrity. In their work, they report that great leaders also cultivate tension by committing to what matters most, including facing any development gaps.[4] The professor side of me likes to keep coming back to key reference points throughout our journey. As we think about the situational impact on communication, recall the following:

> *"Situational moments of impact—every day, every conversation— generate from a place of trust and truth to drive higher performance."*

Fluency in Conversations

Everyone is on a language journey. You're involved with some form of communication every day, whether you're speaking, listening, reading, or writing. *Fluency is the flow of one's speech.* It stems from the Latin word *fluere*, which means "to flow." With that context in mind, you can understand what language fluency is in relation to how words sound as they leave your mouth. Keep in mind that fluency isn't a state you can suddenly achieve. There's a range of fluency, so someone can be highly fluent, hardly fluent, or somewhere in between at any given time in their experiences. We must be continuously investing in our communication fluency so that we can be more fluent both at home and at work.

Proficiency in Conversations

> *"Proficiency refers to one's ability to use language in a spontaneous, unrehearsed context at a given time. In other words, language proficiency describes your level of precision when using and understanding language."*

To summarize, the major difference when comparing fluency and proficiency is that fluency deals with the smoothness of one's speech, while proficiency pertains to the ability to communicate accurately.

In July 2023, Sara Canaday wrote an article in *Psychology Today* titled "Situational Fluency, Exploring the Secret Sauce of Leadership," where she references that situational fluency in communication is a "competitive advantage that separates good leaders from great leaders," and I wholeheartedly agree. She goes on to reference the need to become a world-class observer, listen on a deeper level, customize your communications, and stay flexible." If we as leader/coaches can do this, we will be "able to read the room and adapt to improve communication and connection."[5] As we discussed in early chapters, both personal connection and professional credibility are key elements in building trust in our relationships.

Situational Fluency

In 2021, I wrote a blog titled "Master the Playbook: Situational Fluency," where I defined situational fluency as the ability to engage in a two-way conversation with a deep understanding of context, a natural flow, and a balance between task and relationship. This kind of fluency allows both parties to adapt in real time, helping to solve problems, drive decision-making, manage change, and elevate performance.[6]

Let's look at another version of playbook and situational mastery. Patrick Mahomes of the Kansas City Chiefs is often referred to as a modern-day phenom as a quarterback within the National Football League. According to most analysts, Patrick may already be a Hall of Fame quarterback as he has won three Super Bowl titles, three Super Bowl MVP awards, and two league Most Valuable Player Awards—and he is only twenty-nine at the time of this publication.

Patrick was explaining in an article back in February of 2023 that he feels he needs to remaster the playbook every season, but then his coach, Andy

Reid, will add more layers and depth to those plays throughout a season, showing that his teaching never stops.[7] Coach Reid can only add more layers, however, because Patrick is able to be *situationally fluent* with the base playbook. Unfortunately for most of us, we may not have a base coaching playbook that works! Thus, we go into conversations and just wing it and may lose opportunities for impact. Think back to Jeff's first story at the beginning of the book, where he realized he lost an opportunity for impact.

Here's an important point—situational fluency rarely happens *without* the base playbook first being understood. It goes back to the science; when we're thinking, it's hard to just let go and do. Patrick's depth of the playbook allows him to become fluent in constantly evolving situations that allow him to adapt, adjust, measure progress, perform at a high level, and reach his individual and team goals.

Rigidity at first opens up flexibility later.

So what can you learn from this Super Bowl MVP about situational fluency?

1. Learn & master the playbook (situational conversations – 6P's).
2. Rehearse the plays in your mind (visualize success).
3. Practice the plays (repetition is key).
4. Play multiple scenarios in your mind (before the conversation).
5. Activate the conversation (stop thinking and start doing).
6. Be fully present in every conversation.
7. Be flexible to adjust to in-conversation changes.
8. Adjust as needed.
9. Actively seek feedback versus pushing feedback.
10. Never stop learning—coaching growth never stops.

Situational fluency is the ability to engage in a two-way conversation with deep contextual awareness, natural flow, and a balance between task and relationship. It's the skill that allows leaders to adapt in real time, solve problems, manage change, and drive decisions—all while building trust and alignment. Consider how Patrick Mahomes approaches his role as quarterback. Each season, he remasters the playbook so that his coach, Andy Reid, can build upon it with new layers and complexity. This ongoing evolution is only possible because Patrick has mastered the fundamentals. He doesn't just know the plays—he embodies them, allowing him to adjust, adapt, and elevate in the most dynamic moments. Most of us, however, don't walk into coaching conversations with a well-worn playbook. And without that foundation, our ability to navigate complexity with clarity becomes compromised.

If we consider this situational fluency within the mountain climbing analogy we've been using, it would look like a mountain guide communicating with a climber in shifting terrain. The guide has to read the environment, adjust plans on the fly, and offer real-time insight that keeps the team moving forward. This is what great leaders do with their teams—they read the moment, speak with clarity, and drive progress through every decision point.

Just like a quarterback leading all eleven players on the field or a mountain guide directing a climber, a leader must be attuned to the environment and communicate with precision. When situational fluency is built on a foundation of shared vision, aligned mission, and trust, it becomes the catalyst for a flourishing coaching climate. The climb becomes clearer, the summit more achievable, and the journey one that transforms everyone involved.

Top NeuroCoaching Takeaways

1. **Understand the FOBO paradox in leadership.**

   Many leaders still struggle with situational fluency in conversations, even in today's digital age. Even as technology transforms the workplace, leadership remains fundamentally about influence, dialogue, and collaboration.

2. **Balance task and relationship in communication.**

   Effective leaders adjust their communication styles based on context, ensuring they aren't overly task-focused at the expense of relationships. The best leaders can balance efficiency with connection to build lasting trust and engagement.

3. **Recognize the role of transparency in coaching.**

   Coaching is most effective when leaders share their frameworks and processes openly with their teams. By making coaching transparent and collaborative, leaders can foster trust, engagement, and accountability.

4. **Situational fluency requires a strong foundation.**

   The ability to navigate conversations effectively comes from mastering a base framework first. Like Patrick Mahomes mastering the Chiefs' playbook before adapting on the field, leader/coaches need a structured foundation before they can be flexible in real-time conversations.

CHAPTER 9

CREATING A FLOURISHING COACHING CLIMATE

IMAGINE THIS: A disengaged employee leaves your office after yet another unproductive meeting—their shoulders are slumped, their eyes avoid contact, and the spark that once lit up team meetings feels long extinguished. Their ideas remain unspoken, their talents underutilized, and their motivation and engagement fading by the day. You wonder what else you could possibly say to bring them back to life.

Now, picture a different scene: That same employee walks out of your office energized, notebook (or iPad or reMarkable, depending on your generation or preference) in hand, a clear plan in mind, and the confident body language of someone who knows they belong. Their ideas were heard, their perspective was valued, and they feel a renewed sense of purpose. They're already thinking of how to apply what you discussed.

What changed? A single, intentional coaching conversation that tapped into who they are and what they need to thrive—unlocking their potential in the process.

Every interaction you have as a leader creates a ripple effect—not just on performance, but on morale, innovation, and the emotional tone your team members carry every day. A positive coaching climate is one where individuals feel supported, valued, and motivated to perform at their best.

It's not about adding more to your plate; it's about approaching everyday interactions with intention and purpose.

As we've discussed throughout this book, the NeuroCoaching formula should be becoming clearer: Shared Vision + Aligned Mission + Situational Conversations = Coaching Climate. When this equation is applied consistently and with care, it doesn't just change individual conversations—it transforms the environment.

Thriving coaching climates are the result of leaders who deliberately shape the environment in which their teams operate, where people are empowered, heard, and encouraged to bring their best selves to work. These climates are built on:

- **Clarity:** Clear communication of vision and expectations.
- **Support:** Providing resources, encouragement, and feedback.
- **Trust:** Building authentic relationships through empathy and active listening.

A cornerstone of this climate is the **Situational Conversation**—a flexible, purposeful discussion designed to meet people where they are. When executed well, these conversations unlock performance, increase engagement, and strengthen relationships.

The data is compelling: employees who feel supported by their managers are 70% more likely to be engaged at work.[1] Yet over 60% report that their leaders rarely provide meaningful coaching. That gap is an opportunity—a call to action.

To illustrate this, consider a client story. An executive I coached reached into their desk and pulled out a printed report of their top five strengths. The paper was pristine, and it didn't appear to have been accessed for years. This leader had the tools but wasn't applying them consistently. Contrast that with the leadership training I conduct at the Center for Business Leadership, where over 30 fellows each semester learn to articulate their top values, understand the personal stories that inform those values, activate their emotional intelligence and strengths, and define a clear leadership why. When these students graduate, they leave prepared not just to lead, but to serve. We encourage our students and clients to recognize that we can have the right tools for the mission—but if they're not used, they grow rusty just like relationships, making it harder to survive the storms.

How to Create a Thriving Coaching Climate

1. **Understand the Foundational Pillars**

    - **Employee Vision:** Learn each team member's values, stories, and standards.
    - **Leader Vision:** Clarify your own leadership purpose.
    - **Organizational Vision:** Align your team's goals with broader organizational strategy and people development philosophy.
    - **Aligned Mission:** Strategy, standards, and strengths.
    - **Coaching Effectiveness:** Strengthen your communication to drive sustainable performance with an intentional conversation approach (purpose, perspective, plan/path, progress, problems, performance).

- **Climate Amplifiers:** Emotional intelligence, active listening, psychological safety, organizational awareness, and the emerging impact of VR/AR and AI can all amplify or dampen your coaching climate.

2. **Engage in Intentional Conversations**
    - Ask thoughtful, context-aware questions.
    - Tailor your style to the individual.
    - Be fully present.

3. **Activate Insights with Assessments**
    - Leverage tools like CliftonStrengths, ESCI, and our proprietary Coaching Climate Assessment®.
    - Make yearly assessments a leadership habit.

But knowing is not enough. Action drives change. Over the next 30 days, commit to having one intentional coaching conversation with each team member. Start with:

"What's one thing I can do to help you thrive this week?"

Take a moment and answer these sample questions using the following scale: never, rarely, sometimes, often, consistently. If you want to learn more, please visit us at www.braintrustgrowth.com.

1. My manager can articulate my values.
2. My manager understands their strengths and uses them to help our organization.
3. My manager communicates the company's organizational values.
4. My manager builds unique and independent relationships with each team member.
5. My manager considers my perspective when we engage in conversations.

6. My manager senses others' feelings and perspectives.

7. My manager is fully present in our conversations.

Remember: Coaching climates aren't built overnight. They are cultivated daily. This is not theory; this is lived truth.

Set a reminder for one month from now. Hold yourself accountable—because the best leaders don't just plan to make an impact, they take action.

One of the best practices you can do is assess your coaching climate once a year. You may ask, "Why would I do that?" The answer's simple: change is a constant theme in our journeys. We have new team members, adjusting business cycles, volatile market dynamics, and unexpected climate forces that never—and I mean never—stand still. The tool then becomes part of your compass for team dynamics annually.

As you take this step, remember:

- Leadership isn't about perfection—it's about progress.

- Coaching climates are built daily through consistent, intentional actions.

I've seen this impact not only my students and clients but also myself, so I believe this should be a movement in education and organizational life.

Assessments don't make the magic in leadership; activation does.

Take these elements listed below as a guide when assessing. Unlike the leader who had to pull out their sheet of top strengths as a reminder, every leader needs to have these memorized—activated with a plan to keep them on the path to success—and understand these elements when it comes to the people they lead or the people they influence.

Believe me: using these tools as a compass for you and your team will help guide everyone to deeper conversations, better decision-making, problem-solving, and performance.

You need to know the key elements of your leadership DNA (here is a sample):

- **Personal Values:** Faith, Family, Adventure, Health, Achievement
- **Strengths:** Achiever, Communication, Positivity, Woo, Maximizer
- **Emotional Intelligence:** Emotional self-awareness, self-management, social awareness, relationship management
- **Leader Why:** To help others coach with impact and purpose to build better relationships. Your 'why' needs to be clear, and you must also understand the 'why' of each of your team members.
- **Climate Development Needs:** Employee vision, questioning, and active listening

When activated, these elements serve as a compass for deeper conversations and more informed decisions.

If you already know these for yourself, you're in rare air. Now imagine that clarity across your entire team and organization.

Here's a metaphor: your team is a campfire. When cared for, it provides light, warmth, and energy. Left alone, it either burns out or becomes destructive. Your role is to be the caretaker—stoking the flame, clearing the brush, and re-sparking the fire when it dims.

And if the coaching climate were a mountain expedition, you'd be the guide. The air gets thinner as the goals rise higher. The team relies on your preparation, ability to read the weather, and your instincts when the terrain changes. Some days, you're blazing trails. On other days, you remind others to rest, hydrate, and stay connected to the mission. In both calm and storm, climate shapes whether the summit is reached or abandoned.

The climate you create today will shape tomorrow's fulfillment and performance.

Let's Talk Amplifiers and Dampeners

Much like environmental climate change, we must ask: are we, as leaders, damaging our coaching climate through neglect, misunderstanding, or lack of emotional presence? The United Nations defines climate change as the long-term shifts in temperature and weather patterns. Since the 1800s, "human activities have been the main driver of climate change".[2] Let's look at this through a leadership coaching climate lens. Are we humans damaging the coaching climate between ourselves and our team members? Do we have relationship droughts personally and professionally? Do we have relational scarcity? Are we creating unnecessary fires or dust storms in our relationships?

Watch for warning signs: low engagement, high turnover, and poor communication. These are symptoms of a poor climate.

We must look seriously at our coaching climate, and just like the weather, it can change in every conversation.

Just like in the hit Apple TV series *Ted Lasso*,[3] which follows an American football coach unexpectedly hired to lead an English Premier League soccer team, every coach on the staff shaped the team's climate. Despite having no experience in the sport, Ted's optimism, curiosity, and commitment to people over performance become a catalyst for change. Over time, the coaching staff evolves into a team of diverse strengths and perspectives, each contributing to the emotional dynamics and culture of the club.

Each coach brought something vital to the team's emotional weather—demonstrating the many facets of NeuroCoaching, including a shared vision, an aligned mission, situational conversations, and a constantly shifting climate of storming, norming, and performing. If you've seen the series, you probably noticed the BELIEVE sign hung proudly over the wall leading into their office. If you think about the coaches, each of them brought something unique to the organization that impacted the relationships and the team's performance. Ted (head coach) brought positivity, curiosity, relational energy, vision, culture, and emotional contagion to his players and staff. Ted set the tone. Contrast him with his sidekick, Beard (coach), who was a stoic, trusted confidant who embraced strategy, tactics, and the history of the game. Beard was well-read and added a more transactional balance to Ted.

One thing I loved about their relationship was they were in it together, and nothing was going to split them apart.

As the series went on, we saw the growth of Nate, another coach who was a quiet thinker but also a rising star strategist. It was Ted who saw his potential from day one. Nate needed affirmation but, deep down, was a servant leader seeking to fit in. He was also an example of a young man who, through the need for affirmation, became power-hungry and eventually left the club for a fierce rival. In the end, his loyalty won out, and he returned home as a servant leader.

Rounding out the staff was Coach Roy, an amazing athlete who retired from the game and, as he searched for his place, realized it was back on the field as a coach. Roy knew how to execute the plan while having a hard exterior with a soft inner core. He listened and enforced discipline in the organization. Look at the following graphic, and you'll see that each coach brought their uniqueness to the staff and team. On the surface, it might not appear to be a team that would gel and have success, yet they did. Never be fooled by what's on the surface. Each member of your staff impacts the climate and the dynamics of the team.

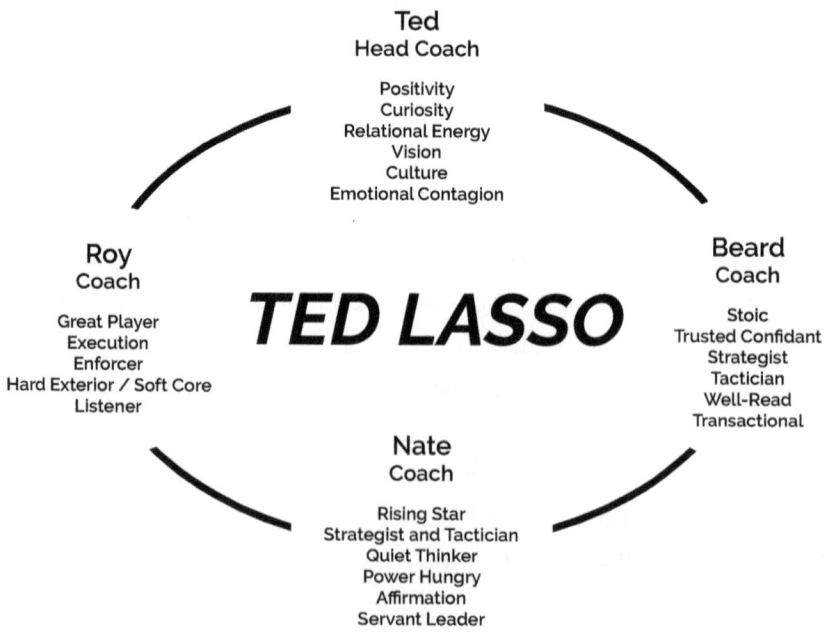

And sometimes, your biggest climate lesson comes in unexpected places. When my son, Drew, was growing up, my wife and I quickly noticed he had excellent hand-eye coordination. I'd spend countless nights throwing a football in the living room, where the carpet served as the field and the hardwood floors were out-of-bounds. Whether it was indoors or out in the snowy backyard, we cherished those moments. Eventually, Drew found his way into Youth Football, where he played from first to sixth grade under Coach Jason, who resembled more of Coach Roy than Coach Ted—a passionate, high-intensity leader who treated youth football like a college program. Four practices a week and Saturday games became our norm. I even became an assistant coach, though my unofficial title was the 'Team Mom on the field.' My job? Ensure the kids are ready—hydrated, warmed up, and focused. During games, I was the first on the field when a player was down. I'd lift them up, dust them off, and get them back in the game. I wasn't calling plays or designing defenses—I was building trust and emotional safety on the sideline.

Over those years, I witnessed how even in youth football, climate amplifiers like emotional intelligence, communication, and role clarity played a significant role. Drew primarily played quarterback on offense and cornerback on defense. As a quarterback, he had natural leadership instincts. He loved learning the game, Mom running plays in the family room, and showed instincts to perform under pressure. He thrived in the position of responsibility.

Two particular situational conversations between Coach Jason and Drew stand out as lasting climate moments, each illustrating how questioning, presence, and metaphor can shape a young leader's mindset:

1. During summer camp, Coach Jason was running plays with the offense. During one practice, he came over to Drew, looked through his facemask, and asked, "Are you going to be with me all year?" Drew, caught off guard, didn't answer. So the coach asked again—this time with more intensity—"Are you going to be with

me all year?" Sweat dripping, Drew nodded vigorously. Later that day, as we got in the car, Drew turned to me and said, "Dad, where does Coach think I'm going?" I laughed and explained that Coach Jason wasn't asking about his physical location, but rather about his focus—his mental presence and commitment. It was a simple question with a profound coaching intent.

2. After another hot summer practice, Coach Jason walked beside Drew with his arm draped around his shoulder pads. He said, "If you want the corner office, you have to act like it." Then he followed up with a question, "Drew, do you want the corner office?" Drew replied, "Yes, Coach, I do!" But in the car afterward, Drew turned to me again and asked, "What's a corner office, and why do I want one?" Once again, the opportunity for a coaching conversation unfolded. We talked about responsibility, leadership, and what it means to show up like a leader long before you hold the title.

These moments may seem small, but they form the foundation of a coaching climate and culture. My wife and I thoroughly enjoyed watching #38 play (I know, an odd number for a quarterback). They're reminders that whether we're coaching young athletes, corporate teams, or emerging leaders, how we engage matters.

Let these tools be your compass. Internalize them. Share them. Build a culture around them. Coaching climates thrive not through grand gestures but through consistent, intentional actions. Every moment matters.

When leaders show up with clarity, empathy, and curiosity, the ripple effect is undeniable. Let your leadership be the spark that ignites a lasting fire.

Ultimately, the best leaders don't just manage; they lead and coach. They create moments and movements within the culture that allow people to flourish and grow.

In the upcoming chapters, we will delve deeper into the following climate amplifiers and dampeners: Leadership Styles, Emotional

Intelligence, NeuroQuestioning, Active Listening, Psychological Safety, Organizational Awareness (power, politics, and influence), and Artificial Intelligence.

Top NeuroCoaching Takeaways

1. **Climate is cultivated, not assumed.**

   Every conversation and interaction contributes either to or detracts from your coaching climate. Leadership presence and consistency matter.

2. **Intentional situational conversations create impact.**

   When leaders engage with purpose, listen actively, and ask thoughtful questions, they unlock growth and performance in others.

3. **Know and activate your leadership DNA.**

   Understanding your own values, strengths, and leadership style is the first step toward modeling and shaping a coaching culture that others will follow.

4. **The coaching climate is shaped by leadership behavior.**

   A leader's style directly influences team engagement, morale, and performance. Just as *Ted Lasso's* coaching staff had different strengths that shaped their team's climate, leaders must recognize how their actions-whether positive or negative-affect their teams' culture and effectiveness.

5. **Great coaching requires thoughtful questioning and clear communication.**

   Just like my son, Drew, how questions are framed can impact understanding and motivation. Effective coaches ask *purposeful, context-driven* questions that inspire clarity, commitment, and action from their team members.

CHAPTER 10

COACHING CLIMATE AMPLIFIERS: LEADERSHIP STYLES & EMOTIONAL INTELLIGENCE

Anyone can become angry—that is easy. But to be angry with the right person, to the right degree, at the right time, for the right purpose, and in the right way—that is not easy.

—Aristotle

AS WE MOVE from establishing a shared vision, aligned mission, and mastering situational conversations, it's critical to recognize the forces that amplify—or dampen—the impact of coaching. Sustainable change doesn't happen in a vacuum; it thrives in a climate intentionally shaped by leadership behaviors, emotional intelligence, and a deep understanding of team dynamics. The way leaders show up, the questions they ask, how actively they listen, and the psychological safety they foster all contribute to whether coaching becomes a catalyst for growth or merely a fleeting interaction. In this next section, we'll explore the essential coaching amplifiers that drive long-term success, as well as the common dampeners that can derail progress. By sharpening skills in leader styles, emotional intelligence, strategic questioning, active listening, psychological safety, and organizational awareness, leaders can elevate coaching from a transactional activity to a transformational force within their teams and organizations.

Before we dive deeper into the idea of climbing the mountain of coaching success, I want to share a moment that brought this "mountain is coaching" metaphor to life in a way I didn't expect. It was during one of the most unforgettable concerts I've ever attended—an evening with Grammy and Dove Award-winning artist Steven Curtis Chapman. The music was powerful and the production flawless, but what left the greatest impression on me was how Steven navigated the stage—not just musically, but relationally. His ability to adapt, connect, and lead the audience through both celebration and reflection reminded me that success isn't just about reaching the summit; it's about how we climb, who we bring with us, and how we show up along the way. The performance was a mastery in songwriting, producing, and musical prowess, but what really stood out to me was Steven's ability to shift communication style during his performance.

Steven Curtis Chapman has been a defining figure in contemporary Christian music for over three decades. Emerging in the late 1980s, he quickly became known for his heartfelt lyrics, blending elements of pop and rock with messages of faith and hope. With a career spanning multiple generations, he has released numerous albums and continues to inspire audiences with his music. His ability to craft songs that speak to both personal struggles and spiritual journeys has made him one of the most beloved artists in Christian music history.

Chapman's impact is reflected in his record-breaking success. He has won over fifty Dove Awards, more than any other artist, and has received five Grammy Awards in various gospel categories. With more than eleven million albums sold and forty-nine number one hits on the Christian music charts, his influence is undeniable. His songs, such as "Cinderella," "Dive," and "Speechless," have resonated deeply with listeners, reinforcing his reputation as a storyteller who brings faith to life through music.

Beyond his musical accomplishments, Chapman and his wife, Mary Beth, have dedicated their lives to philanthropy through their organization, Show Hope. Founded to help orphans find permanent families, Show Hope provides financial assistance to families navigating the adoption process. The organization has grown to include medical care, pre-adoption support, and advocacy efforts, expanding its reach to children around the world. Chapman's commitment to this cause, deeply personal to his family, reflects his broader mission to use his platform for lasting impact beyond the stage.

As an artist, Steven's versatility was on full display throughout the concert as he seamlessly transitioned between different guitars, a piano, and even percussion, all while sharing heartfelt stories, engaging with his tour companions, and opening up about his personal journey in life and music. However, one might recognize a parallel from this concert with that of leadership coaching by the necessity of versatility and adaptability on full display.

Just as a musician like Steven can adjust his performance to engage the audience, a coach must adjust their leadership style to engage the team. A single style cannot fit all circumstances. Just as a high-energy musical piece differs significantly from a slower-tempo ballad, the emotions and techniques required in coaching must be varied to meet diverse challenges.

One last note about this amazing concert. Had we not been there that evening, we may never have felt the call to pursue the dream of adoption. One moment in time lit a spark that would eventually lead us down the path to adoption to the amazing day when we brought our youngest daughter home from China. We were blessed to get the opportunity to once again see Steven in concert with our daughter and Kayla, where we could thank him for the impact of a single moment in time. As a coach, you have this same opportunity for impact every day.

Adaptability in Leadership

When you think of yourself in different situations, how do you show versatility and adaptability? Think of a leader that you've worked for and ask yourself if they demonstrated the ability to adapt styles based on ever-changing environments around them. Did they adapt well in times of an organizational structure change, a large company expansion, the changing of a high-level C-suite executive, or a sudden budget change? You could list thousands of scenarios where you or the leader/coach you're thinking of weren't able to adjust.

Adaptability in leadership is fundamental in nurturing a robust coaching environment where support, guidance, and inspiration are paramount. This versatility is essential as it recognizes the need for varied leadership approaches to effectively meet the disparate needs of situations, teams, and individuals within the coaching landscape.

If we're adaptable, we allow for the accommodation of diverse personalities and learning styles. In any team, individuals vary in their responses to different types of leadership. Some may thrive under a directive approach, while others may excel when given more autonomy. A leader who can flexibly switch between styles can effectively engage with each team member in the most beneficial manner.[1] This personalized approach not only boosts individual performance but also contributes to a more cohesive and efficient team dynamic. If we think back to our prior chapters, leader-member exchange theory demonstrates that we need to form unique independent relationships with each of our team members. To activate this, we must be able to adjust our styles.

Moreover, the modern workplace is characterized by constant change, whether in people, technology, market demands, or organizational structures. Leaders who're adaptable in their coaching styles are better equipped to guide their teams through these changes. They can shift their focus and strategies in response to new challenges, helping their team to remain relevant and competitive. This flexibility also sets an example for team members, encouraging them to be adaptable and resilient in the face of change. I'm convinced after thirty years in business that people will "re-model" what you model.

In addition, adaptability in leadership styles is crucial for fostering a culture of continuous learning and development.[2] We're friends with the Blanchard company, and this premise of a leader/coach adjusting style while processing the situational readiness of each team member is what helps leader-member exchange (LMX) and situational leadership (SLII°) stand the test of time. The leadership styles range from directing to coaching to supporting to delegating (S1-S4) by also considering the developmental needs from low competence to high competence (D1-D4) at a task level. At the heart of SLII is awareness and adaptability.[3]

Leaders who adapt their styles also excel in conflict resolution—which, let me tell you, is difficult to master. Different conflicts require different approaches; some might need a more authoritative intervention, while others could be better resolved through collaborative problem-solving. An adaptable leader can assess the situation and apply the most effective conflict resolution strategy, maintaining team harmony and productivity. The root of constructive versus destructive conflict is emotions and a poor ability to control them.[4]

When leaders adjust their approach to suit their team members' preferences and needs, it demonstrates a genuine concern for their well-being and professional growth. This can lead to increased job satisfaction, higher morale, and, consequently, greater employee retention. In an era when talent retention is crucial, adaptable leadership can be a significant asset.

So you can see why an adaptable leadership style in coaching is essential for promoting innovation and creativity. Leaders who can adjust their coaching style to foster an environment that encourages innovation while also providing the necessary support and guidance can drive their teams toward groundbreaking ideas and solutions.

Take the Korn Ferry group, for example; they found that effective leaders have up to six dimensions of climate that impact performance—clarity (people know what is expected), standards (challenging but attainable goals), flexibility (no unnecessary rules and procedures), responsibility (people are empowered with accountability), rewards (good performance is recognized and rewarded), and team commitment (people are proud to belong and collaborate).[5] Leader/coaches who can maximize each of these dimensions are able to have sustainable performance.

Resonant and Dissonant Leadership Styles

"50–70 percent of the variance in team climate can be explained by differences in leadership style."[6]

If you research, you can find multiple variations of leadership styles, but we advocate for the styles published within *Primal Leadership*. I've not only had the opportunity to learn about these styles directly from Dr. Boyatzis but I have consulted with him on how to integrate and activate this knowledge into undergraduate, graduate, and consulting environments. It has been a pleasure to train this concept to thousands of students and organizational leaders, but each time we train, the participants walk away with the same conclusion: It isn't just about the style; it's about how we adapt our styles and intentionally flex in varying situations. The best leaders can do this, and those who can't are the equivalent of playing only one chord on a guitar. It simply isn't enough.

Think of these styles as resonant and dissonant. In *Primal Leadership*, resonance in the human analog is that "a synchronous vibration occurs when two people are on the same wavelength emotionally—when they feel in sync. Resonance amplifies and prolongs the emotional impact of leadership."[7] The resonant styles include visionary, participative, coaching, and affiliative. Let's take a closer look.

Visionary – Builds resonance by *moving people toward shared dreams*; impact on climate is mainly positive; it's appropriate when changes require a new vision or when a clear direction is needed.

Coaching – Builds resonance by *connecting what a person wants with the team's* and organization's standards and goals; impact on climate is highly positive; it is appropriate to help an employee improve performance by building long-term capabilities.

Affiliative – Builds resonance by *creating harmony in connecting people* to each other; impact on climate is positive; it is appropriate when you need to heal rifts in a team, motivate during stressful times, or strengthen connections.

Democratic – Builds resonance by *valuing people's input while getting commitment* through participation; impact on climate is positive; it is appropriate when building buy-in or consensus or getting valuable input from team members.

Now, really pay attention here: Dissonance in *Primal Leadership* refers to "a lack of harmony. Dissonant leadership produces groups that feel emotionally discordant, in which people have a sense of being continually off-key."[8] We've all experienced this at least once or twice in our jobs. The dissonant styles include pacesetting and commanding. The styles can be effective in the short-term, but there should be caution if they are overused, are your only dominant style, or you lack the self-awareness to overuse or the ability to adapt.

Pacesetting – Although a dissonant style, it can build resonance when meeting challenging and exciting goals; if not executed well, it often has a highly negative impact on climate; it is appropriate when needing to get high-quality results from a motivated and competent team.

Commanding – Although a dissonant style, it can build resonance when it soothes fears by giving clear direction in an emergency; because it is frequently misused, it often has a highly negative impact on climate; it is appropriate when in a crisis to kick-start change or a turnaround.

Coaching Tip to Activate

Effective leadership coaching and style adaptations are like being a skilled musician or orienteer in the ever-changing turbulence of the workplace. Adaptability of styles is the compass that keeps you on course. At our Center for Business Leadership, we use a compass as a guiding image when working with our leadership fellows on how to lead on purpose. In order to foster an environment where your team can thrive, it's essential to recognize that one size doesn't fit all. Again, your team is diverse, and each member may require a different approach.

Here's a coaching tip: Think of your leadership style as a toolkit. Sometimes, a situation calls for the hammer of a *commanding* style, while at other times, the screwdriver of a *democratic* style is necessary. So be observant. Notice how your team responds to different styles at different times and adjust accordingly. If you're fully present at work, you might notice that the environment may change within the hour and be caused by multiple factors.

For instance, when facing tight deadlines, a more *pacesetting* style might be needed to ensure efficiency. Conversely, during brainstorming sessions for new projects, an *affiliative* approach can spark creativity and investment in the ideas generated.[9]

Embrace the learning curve that comes with adapting your style. It might feel uncomfortable at first, but with practice, it can become second nature, just like a guitarist strumming different chords from song to song.

Remember, the goal of adaptability in leadership is not to change who you are but to become versatile in how you lead, ensuring your team not only succeeds but excels.

> The goal of adaptability in leadership is not to change who you are but to become versatile in how you lead, ensuring your team not only succeeds but excels.

One last tip: Adopt a policy of no secrets with your team (unless mandated by the organization) and have transparency in your leadership style. Here's a brief example:

Exercise to Activate

This exercise will help you think outside yourself while activating the principles of leader/coach styles.

1. Recommend reading *Primal Leadership*.
2. Select a leadership style that is interesting to you and complete a Google or Safari search to learn more about that style. You may want to choose one that isn't natural for you.
3. Select a leader profile that you think best represents the style [i.e., Steve Jobs – Visionary].
4. Overview the organization where he or she led [Apple – Transition from Steve Jobs to Tim Cook].
5. Analyze how the leader adapted their style [incorporate at least one other style – i.e., Steve Jobs after being fired from Apple only to return for a second run].
6. Reflect on your dominant leadership style and challenge yourself to determine how you adapt in different situations. Be specific and journal an example.

Emotional Intelligence

If there could only be one area of investment in a team of leaders, I'd put it all toward a foundation of coaching and emotional intelligence (EI).[10] The opportunity to work with a thought leader in this space is something I will never forget or take for granted. As I became certified in emotional intelligence, it became apparent that this had to be the number one amplifier or dampener when it came to the coaching climate.

At Braintrust, we reviewed several emotional intelligence certifications, and we realized it would be most beneficial to be certified in and offer our clients the Emotional Social Competency Inventory (ESCI) that was developed by my mentor Dr. Richard Boyatzis and Dr. Daniel Goleman, now owned by Korn Ferry.[11]

As a leader/coach, it's imperative that you have this foundational training; however, even more important is the ability to strategize how to gameplan your strengths and bring awareness to how you can minimize gaps for emotional competencies that aren't the strongest.

In this section, we'll learn how to effectively activate and define EI and competency and describe the critical emotional competencies within ESCI.

Before we jump in, though, I'd like to share a quote from Aristotle, featured in the epigraph for this chapter, that'll help us frame how EI isn't a new concept. Aristotle said, "Anyone can become angry—that's easy. But to be angry with the right person, to the right degree, at the right time, for the right purpose, and in the right way—this is not easy."[12] So it's clear that emotional intelligence and the impact of self-management of emotion aren't new. But if you don't want to take Aristotle's word for it, then consider a report from the World Economic Forum that cited emotional intelligence as one of the top ten skills needed for professional success in 2020 and beyond.[13]

Take it a step further in another World Economic Forum article, written in collaboration with Adam Grant:

"[there's] no connection between IQ and emotional intelligence; you simply can't predict EI based on how smart someone is . . . EI is a flexible set of skills that can be acquired and improved with practice."[14]

Since the 1990s, emotional intelligence (EI) has been a part of leadership vernacular around the business world and is at the core of how we lead. The good news for leaders is that it's not just an innate trait—it can be learned.[15] EI domains and associated emotional competencies are divided into personal and social competencies. Personal competencies are how we manage ourselves with self-awareness and self-management, while social competencies are how we manage relationships, which include empathy and developing others.[16]

There are decades of research supporting EI. If you want support for performance, "TalentSmart tested EI alongside thirty-three other important workplace skills and found that emotional intelligence is the strongest predictor of performance, explaining a full 58 percent of success in all types of jobs."[17]

Think of it this way: Change driven by fear isn't long-lasting, but change driven by hopes and aspirations can endure.[18] The gap: How do we move emotional competencies from an understanding of importance to subconscious competence in the everyday habits of coaches where it becomes second nature?

With over twenty-five years of research, the ESCI model has four primary quadrants that can aid in better understanding emotional competency and are worth learning:

Self-awareness: Recognizing and understanding our own emotions.

Self-management: Effectively managing our own emotions.

Social awareness: Recognizing and understanding others' emotions.

Relationship management: Applying emotional understanding in our dealings with others.

Inside each of these quadrants are twelve competencies, and I feel it's important to understand and define these:

Self-awareness

- Emotional self-awareness: The ability to understand our own emotions and their effects on our performance.

Self-management

- Emotional self-control: The ability to keep disruptive emotions and impulses in check and maintain our effectiveness under stressful or hostile conditions.
- Achievement orientation: Striving to meet or exceed a standard of excellence; looking for ways to do things better, setting challenging goals, and taking calculated risks.
- Positive outlook: The ability to see the positive in people, situations, and events and our persistence in pursuing goals despite obstacles and setbacks.
- Adaptability: Flexibility in handling change, juggling multiple demands and adapting our ideas or approaches.

Social Awareness

- Empathy: The ability to sense others' feelings and perspectives, taking an active interest in their concerns and picking up cues to what is being felt and thought.
- Organizational awareness: The ability to read a group's emotional currents and power relationships, identifying influencers, networks, and dynamics.

Relationship Management

- Influence: The ability to have a positive impact on others, persuading or convincing others to gain their support.

- Coach and mentor: The ability to foster the long-term learning or development of others by giving feedback and support.

- Conflict management: The ability to help others through emotional or tense situations, tactfully bringing disagreements into the open and finding solutions all can endorse.

- Inspirational leadership: The ability to inspire and guide individuals and groups to get the job done and to bring out the best in others.

- Teamwork: The ability to work with others toward a shared goal; participating actively, sharing responsibility and rewards, and contributing to the capacity of the team.

On October 2, 1995, the cover of *Time Magazine* read, "What Is your EQ?" The description read, "It's not your IQ. It's not even a number. But emotional intelligence may be the best predictor of success in life, redefining what it means to be smart."[19] However, in a 2022 *Forbes* article, a study from the Center for Creative Leadership reported that "75 percent of careers derail for reasons relating to emotional competencies. This scenario includes the inability to handle interpersonal problems, unsatisfactory team leadership during times of difficulty or conflict, or the inability to adapt to change or elicit trust."[20] I hope you're quickly seeing the impact of building relationships by unleashing a deeper understanding of your emotional competencies.

Back when I was being certified, there were two competencies that needed attention. My identified strengths were emotional self-awareness, achievement orientation, positive outlook, empathy, and coaching/

mentoring.[21] But let's spend a moment on two growth areas in my report—adaptability and conflict management. It didn't come as a surprise that conflict management was a gap of mine. I haven't enjoyed conflict since I was young. I've never handled it well and have had to coach myself to address it even when it's uncomfortable. But the one that did surprise me was adaptability. I had to take a close examination of my behavior in situations and after being honest with myself and consulting others close to me, I came to the realization that this is, in fact, a growth area. I had to dig deep to think of situations and people that would cause my lack of adaptability. Once I had the awareness, I could develop a strategy to manage it, including asking questions, listening, and changing my mindset in certain situations. Without the knowledge and reflection, I couldn't put a plan in motion to address my growth areas.

So let's discuss a coaching tip for you.

Coaching Tip to Activate

If you take a closer look at the competency definitions, you'll see a significant connection to the elements in the design of Situational Conversations—exceeding standards of excellence, seeing others' feelings and perspectives, the ability to inspire and guide others, and understanding emotions' effects on performance.

If you have never assessed your emotional competencies, I strongly recommend that you make that investment. Once you complete the assessment, find a trained coach to work through the results with you. But if you aren't able to do an assessment, I recommend the following exercise to get you started.

Exercise to Activate

Refer to the four quadrants and competencies.

1. What do you see as strengths and areas of growth?

2. Identify one to three competencies.

3. Think of at least two situations in your personal and professional life.

4. Reflect on your emotions, including what and who triggers those emotions.

5. Discuss your situations and thoughts with a trusted family member, friend, or colleague. Note: Make sure to select someone who will be honest with you.

6. Outline a plan of action for each identified competency.

7. Discuss the plan with an accountability partner.

Here's an example:

1. Area of growth: Emotional self-control.

2. Definition: The ability to keep disruptive emotions and impulses in check and maintain our effectiveness under stressful or hostile conditions.

3. Trigger: When I don't feel appreciated or respected.

4. Plan of action: Sleep on it, do breathing exercises, find dedicated focus time, smile, laugh, and embrace the twenty-four-hour rule before responding.

Another effective approach is to journal your emotions for a week. Select three times a day to write down the emotions you're feeling (9:00 a.m., 12:00 p.m., and 5:00 p.m.). At the end of the day, log your insights from that day. Repeat this for a week and see if you can identify any themes. After that, you can strategize how to proactively address the emotions.

I do this exercise with the MBA students in my leadership coaching class, and the students often comment that they have never done this before and plan to continue in the future. But all of this can be a moot point without an emotional accountability partner who can discuss how you're leveraging and developing your EI growth areas. It's helpful to keep this partner for at least six months.

Top NeuroCoaching Takeaways

1. **Adaptability in leadership is key to effective coaching.**

   A leader must adapt their coaching style to different situations, team members, and challenges. Versatile leaders can create stronger relationships, improve team dynamics, and foster long-term growth.

2. **Leadership styles must be intentional and flexible.**

   The best leaders don't rely on one leadership style but rather shift between *visionary, coaching, affiliative, democratic, pacesetting,* and *commanding* approaches depending on the needs of their team. The ability to flex between resonant and dissonant leadership styles ensures a leader remains effective in various situations.

3. **Emotional intelligence (EI) is a critical leadership skill.**

   EI isn't a soft skill; it plays a significant role in leadership success. Developing self-awareness, self-management, social awareness, and relationship management helps leaders build stronger teams, navigate conflict, and create a positive coaching climate.

CHAPTER 11

COACHING CLIMATE AMPLIFIERS: NEUROQUESTIONING & ACTIVE LISTENING

The greatest compliment that was ever paid me was when someone asked me what I thought and attended to my answer.
—HENRY DAVID THOREAU

WE WELCOMED OUR youngest daughter, Priya, into our family from India when she was two-and-a-half years old. Once she started to become comfortable in her new home, I was reminded of just how profound a toddler's curiosity can be. Yet I soon noticed that Priya's inquisitiveness was distinctly different compared to that of her older siblings, Grace and Drew. As toddlers, Grace and Drew pondered the mysteries of their secure, suburban world with questions like: "Why does the dog have fur, and I don't?" "Why does the moon only appear at night and not during the day like the sun?" "Why do you shout at the TV during football games?" You know... the usual questions.

Priya's questions, however, stemmed from a deeper, more vulnerable place. "Can you promise to sleep with me all night without leaving?" "When is Mommy coming back? She will come back, right?" Her questions echoed a need for assurance, a lingering fear born from her past experiences. In her precious little mind, these were questions of survival. As time passed and Priya felt increasingly secure in the loving embrace of her new environment, her questions began to shift. They evolved from expressions of anxiety and fear to signs of a blossoming curiosity, painting a picture of a young mind eager to explore her world without fear. In this chapter, we'll dive more deeply into two crucial tools that significantly impact your ability to create that productive and safe coaching climate: the art of *asking impactful questions* coupled with the skill of *active listening* aimed at truly understanding.

If you recall from earlier discussions with the hand model of the brain, our innate instinct is self-preservation. It's only when we feel secure that we become receptive to new ideas. As the "sender" of a question, recognizing the importance of being aware of our emotional state and the level of stress we're experiencing is crucial. These factors directly influence not only the nature of the questions we pose but also how we present them and their subsequent impact and interpretation by the "receiver."

When stressed, our brains default to self-preservation. This can make us ask questions from a place of self-interest instead of genuine curiosity. The result? Disengagement and defensiveness instead of real connection. When preoccupied with our own needs (survival) over the receiver's, the questions we pose may, unfortunately, yield results contrary to our intentions. It's vital to strive for a balance, ensuring our inquiries come from a place of empathy and a genuine desire to understand, fostering a more positive and constructive exchange.

The Neuroscience of Asking Impactful Questions

I had the chance to observe a senior leader of one of our top clients recently. He had been through the NeuroCoaching program and was being coached monthly for ongoing support. His team was a melting pot of creativity and innovation with a side serving of dysfunction, unhealthy competition, and possibly a larger-than-average collective set of egos. One of his biggest challenges was aligning his leader vision (which was already aligned with the company vision) to each of their individual visions while at the same time helping them see the power of team collaboration for future success. I was excited to see how he might implement his newfound understanding of neuroscience in their next team meeting.

The meeting began as usual, with the team gathered around a large, oval table, the morning sunlight casting a warm glow through the panoramic windows. He started by asking each member a series of thoughtfully crafted questions designed not just to elicit information but to engage them on a deeper level. "When you think of all the various initiatives you are working on, what aspect of your current project excites you the most?" "If you were to describe to a stranger how this project aligns with your personal goals or interest, how would you do so?" "What unique challenge have you faced on the project so far, and what have you done or are doing about it?"

As the questions flowed, something remarkable started to happen within the brains of the team members. Each question acted like a key, unlocking compartments within their minds that housed emotions, memories, and creative ideas. The empathic network lit up with activity, engaging each member in deep, reflective thought, and you could feel the emotion begin to stir as each team member began attaching personal significance and motivation to their work.

I could tell by the sly, almost prideful grin on his face that he knew his questions acted as a catalyst for both emotional and cognitive engagement. He understood that when the brain engages in such a manner, it releases a cocktail of neurotransmitters. Dopamine, the reward molecule, offered a sense of pleasure and satisfaction with each insightful answer shared. Oxytocin, often associated with trust and bonding, fostered a stronger sense of team cohesion. Even the stress hormone cortisol played a role, lowering in response to the positive, supportive environment, reducing anxiety and opening the doors to creative thinking.

As the meeting progressed, the team members found themselves more openly sharing ideas and insights, building upon each other's thoughts with a synergy previously unseen. The neural networks within their brains, once like isolated islands, now formed bridges, connecting disparate ideas into innovative solutions and strategies.

His approach involving laser-focused, intentional questions did more than just enhance the meeting; it transformed the team's dynamic. The members left the room not just as colleagues but as collaborators who understood and valued each other's perspectives and contributions. The atmosphere in the office shifted, becoming one of excitement, creativity, and mutual respect.

In the following weeks, the team's performance and output exceeded all expectations. Projects that had been stuck in limbo found direction. Innovative solutions emerged for long-standing problems. The team's success caught the attention of the entire company, setting a new standard for collaboration and achievement.

By understanding the neuroscience of asking great questions, he had unlocked a level of performance and satisfaction among his team that was previously unimaginable. This inspired other managers to adopt a similar approach, transforming the company culture from the inside out.

This story illustrates not just the importance of asking good questions as a leader but also the profound impact understanding neuroscience can have on leadership, communication, and organizational success. The brain's response to thoughtfully posed questions is not just a scientific fact but a key to unlocking the full potential of teams and organizations.

As we begin to think more deeply about the "coaching climate" concept all of us have created, either intentionally or unintentionally, I'm reminded of the countless conversations I've had over the years—each one a unique journey into the minds and hearts of those I've had the privilege to coach. Through my work, I've discovered an undeniable truth: The power of a question can unlock the deepest potential within us. And when coupled with the art of listening, well, that's where the real magic happens.

Insightful questions work because they bypass the surface level of conscious thought and tap into the deeper, more reflective parts of the brain. These are the regions where our true desires, fears, and values reside, often unexamined. By asking questions that prompt reflection on these deeper aspects, we invite a journey inward to a place where the real answers lie.

> The power of a question can unlock the deepest potential within us.

From a neuroscience perspective, when faced with a thought-provoking question, the brain engages in a fascinating process. *Instinctive elaboration* refers to an automatic, subconscious process where an individual naturally expands upon new information by linking it to their existing knowledge, experiences, or emotional responses. This cognitive mechanism is innate, driven by the individual's inherent tendencies and past experiences. When encountering new data, the brain instinctively seeks connections with what it already knows or feels, facilitating a deeper understanding and integration of the information into memory. This process enhances learning and memory retention because information that resonates on a personal or emotional level is more likely to be remembered and understood. It's a fundamental aspect of how humans process and internalize new concepts, making learning more efficient and meaningful by utilizing the subconscious mind's ability to make connections and elaborate on new stimuli without deliberate effort. Essentially, when you ask a question, that very act hijacks the receiver's brain and shuts down all other neural processing, leaving active only the areas responsible and necessary for processing and responding to that single thought.

As this focused neural activity increases, neuroplasticity comes into play. This term refers to the brain's ability to form and reorganize synaptic connections, especially in response to learning or experience. Insightful questions, therefore, can literally change the structure of our brain, making us more receptive to new ideas and ways of thinking.

The analogy of planting a seed in fertile soil mirrors the growth mindset. Carol Dweck, a psychologist at Stanford University, introduced this concept to describe the belief that abilities can be developed through dedication and hard work.[1] Insightful questions cultivate this mindset by challenging individuals to think beyond their perceived limitations and explore their potential.

Open-Ended versus Closed-Ended Questions

Let's revisit a concept we're all somewhat acquainted with—the dichotomy of question types. We're talking about open-ended and closed-ended questions, the twin pillars of communication that draw out distinct responses. This brief description is designed to expand our vocabulary of questions, which is critical in communication effectiveness. With a vast array of options at our disposal, skillfully employing open-ended or closed-ended questions becomes a pivotal strategy in our communicative repertoire.

Open-ended impact questions or interrogative questions are those that *can't* be answered with a simple yes or no. These questions require more detailed and thoughtful responses. The purpose of these questions is to encourage a full, meaningful answer using the coachee's own knowledge and feelings. They are useful in exploring feelings, opinions, attitudes, and understanding.

Look at our options below. As you review them, ask yourself how many you utilize and with what frequency.

Who, Why, When, Where, What, Which, Whom, Whose, and How

Let's think back to our situational conversations for an example. This question is designed to be asked between the *plan* and *progress* steps of the coaching conversation framework. "When you think about the plan you developed, how best can I help you measure progress?" This immediately focuses the coachee on the plan and shows you care about helping them measure their progress. In this example, we utilize two open-ended question types—when and how. We call this question stacking with purpose.

This leads us to a very important question-building "formula" that will really help you as you begin evaluating and building questions of your own. When building and delivering great questions, it's imperative that you consider three critical areas: your motivation (M), the question's actual grammatical structure (S), and, finally, your tone of voice in delivery (T).

$$M + S + T = Impact$$

Now, let's look at close-ended impact questions or, rather, auxiliary questions. These are questions that *can* be answered with a simple yes, no, or maybe. They can also be answered with a specific set of options like A, B, C, or D. These questions are designed to be concise and focus on extracting factual information. These question types can help us gather facts, make decisions, or move a conversation along the path. Just because our options for responses are more limited, it doesn't mean that we have our coachee rush the answer. Let the coachee think unless you strategically want a quick answer. If that's the case, you can use the power of your vocal cords through intonation to affect the speed of their response. Once again, we have a great set of options in our questioning vocabulary.

Is, Are, Can, Was, Were, Have, Has, Do, Does, Did

Let's revisit our situational conversations for an example. This question is designed to be asked at the *performance* step of the framework. I'm again going to use a stacking technique to focus the question: "When you think about your yearly performance, did you meet your expectations?" The "when" helps the coachee think about the yearly performance, where the question must elicit a yes, no, or maybe. Now, in this example, I would caution you on your motivation. Why are you asking this question this way? Is it a "gotcha" question where you both know the answer is a resounding no and you are simply going to hit them with a series of "why not" hammers? Closed-ended questions are useful when you need clear, concise answers or when you're simply gauging commitment or understanding. When used incorrectly, they can actually spike cortisol and cause the receiver to put up defenses, both unconsciously and, at times, consciously.

Here is another word of caution: If you don't get the answer you expect with your question, you should have a second question already in the batter's box. If the conversation is stressful, and you don't get the answer you expect, you run the risk of cortisol (stress chemical) taking over, and you won't think as clearly. If the answer is no and you expected a yes, you can return to an open-ended question. For example, you could ask, "Which element of your performance didn't meet your expectations?" And your conversations, your motivation, structure, and tone matter, whether it's a question or not. Recall that every conversation is a situational moment of impact.

The choice between open-ended and closed-ended questions can significantly impact the direction and depth of a conversation. On the one hand, open-ended questions are more exploratory and can lead to a richer, more detailed exchange, making them ideal for interviews, counseling, and coaching settings. Closed-ended questions, on the other hand, are more suited for surveys, quizzes, or when specific, concise information is needed.

Here's a short list of various types of questions that average managers might ask (before) versus those who are steeped in the NeuroCoaching philosophy (after):

Before: "Why do you think you failed?"

After: "As you reflect on this project, what did this experience teach you about your approach, and how might you adjust it moving forward?"

・・・・・・・・・・・・・・・・・・・・・・・・・・・・・・・・

Before: "Why are you always missing your deadlines?"

After: "When you think of all the various tasks you have on your plate, what challenges are you facing with meeting deadlines, and how can we work together to overcome them?"

・・・・・・・・・・・・・・・・・・・・・・・・・・・・・・・・

Before: "Why did you make this mistake again?"

After: "I noticed a recurring issue. What do you think is causing it, and what support do you need to address it?"

・・・・・・・・・・・・・・・・・・・・・・・・・・・・・・・・

Before: "Why don't you get along with your team?"

After: "How do you feel about our team dynamics, and are there ways you think we can improve our collaboration?"

・・・・・・・・・・・・・・・・・・・・・・・・・・・・・・・・

Before: "This work isn't up to our standards. What went wrong?"

After: "Let's talk about how this project turned out. What were your biggest hurdles, and how can we ensure quality moving forward?"

・・・・・・・・・・・・・・・・・・・・・・・・・・・・・・・・

Before: "Don't you think you should be taking more initiative?"

After: "What are some areas where you feel you could have a bigger impact, and what support would you need to take the lead on those?"

· ·

Before: "Have you noticed that you always seem to bring problems instead of solutions?"

After: "When you encounter a problem, let's discuss both the challenge and your ideas for solutions. How can I support you in solving problems more autonomously?"

· ·

Before: "Is there a reason you can't seem to arrive on time?"

After: "I've noticed some challenges with punctuality. Is everything okay, and is there anything we can do to help make it easier for you to arrive on time?"

· ·

Before: "Is there a reason my feedback isn't being implemented?"

After: "I want to ensure the feedback you receive is actionable. What can we do to help you feel more equipped to implement feedback?"

· ·

Before: "Haven't you made any progress on your personal development goals?"

After: "Let's revisit your personal development goals. What obstacles have you encountered, and how can we adjust our approach to support your growth?"

· ·

When you work hard to become unconsciously competent at asking great questions, you will naturally reframe your questions in your mind prior to asking them the wrong way. This not only shifts focus from failure to learning but also stimulates the emotional processing necessary for personal growth.

Timing and context are everything. The effectiveness of an insightful question greatly depends on the receptiveness of the individual and the situation at hand. It's like knowing when the soil is ready for the seed. There's a delicate balance between challenging someone to step out of their comfort zone and providing a safe space for them to explore their thoughts and emotions.

This is where the art of coaching truly shines. It's not just about having a list of powerful questions; it's about knowing your coachee well enough to ask the right question at the right moment. It requires active listening, empathy, and a deep understanding of the individual's current state of mind and emotional landscape.

> There's a delicate balance between challenging someone to step out of their comfort zone and providing a safe space for them to explore their thoughts and emotions.

As we navigate the crossroads of our lives, the most insightful questions are those that turn our gaze inward, prompting us to reflect on our values, aspirations, and the obstacles that hold us back. They encourage us to chart our own course through the dense forest of life's possibilities. In doing so, we not only discover new paths but also unlock the potential within us to journey down them with confidence and purpose.

The power of an insightful question lies in its ability to initiate a process of self-discovery and growth, reflecting the true essence of coaching. By understanding the neuroscience behind this transformative tool, we can better appreciate the profound impact it can have on our personal and professional development.

The Power of Active Listening

Next, let's make no mistake that even the best inquirers in the world at building and delivering great questions are amateurs at communication if they are poor at active listening. The great Stephen Covey once said, "Most people do not listen with the intent to understand; they listen with the intent to reply."[2]

In the chaos of today's overly crowded agendas and the never-ending flow of sensory inputs, the art of listening—truly listening—has become as rare as it is vital. As an author and entrepreneur committed to effective communication and leadership, I've witnessed firsthand the transformative power of active listening. It's not just about hearing the words spoken; it's about understanding the symphony of human emotion and thought beneath them. The neuroscience behind this skill is as fascinating as it is crucial for anyone looking to foster deeper connections, whether in personal relationships or becoming a world-class coach in the professional setting.

Active listening triggers a series of intricate neurological processes. When we listen actively, we engage various parts of the brain, notably the temporal lobes, responsible for processing auditory information, and the empathic network, which plays a key role in attention and empathy. The amygdala, our emotional processing center, lights up, indicating the emotional investment required in genuine listening.

The magic begins in the moment of silence between words. In these gaps, our brains are not idle; they are intensely active, weaving together narratives, emotions, and logical threads from the sounds we receive. This synthesis allows us to grasp not just the *explicit* message conveyed but the *implicit* tones of emotions, intentions, and unspoken thoughts. It's a cognitive dance that demands both attention and *intention*.

Neurologically, active listening enhances the production of neurotransmitters like dopamine and oxytocin, often associated with pleasure, bonding, and trust, respectively. This chemical response not only makes the act of listening rewarding but also fosters a deeper sense of connection between the speaker and the listener. It's a testament to how our brains are wired to connect through the act of listening, underlining the social nature of our species.

The Barriers to Effective Listening

Despite our neurological setup favoring connection, several barriers impede our ability to listen actively. The omnipresence of digital distractions, the stress of multitasking, and the preoccupation with formulating responses while others speak all contribute to a superficial level of listening that barely scratches the surface of understanding.

Moreover, the listener's biases and preconceptions often filter the message, altering its reception. This cognitive distortion, rooted in the brain's natural inclination to confirm existing beliefs, can significantly hinder open and unbiased listening.

Action Steps to Enhance Active Listening

Understanding the importance and benefits of active listening is the first step. Implementing this understanding into actionable strategies is where the real transformation begins. Here are several steps to take:

1. *Create a Listening Environment*: Minimize distractions. Turn off notifications, find a quiet space, and ensure you're physically comfortable. Signal to your brain and the speaker that you're fully present.

2. *Adopt a Learner's Mindset*: Approach each listening opportunity with curiosity and openness. Challenge yourself to learn something new, setting aside preconceived notions and judgments.

3. *Employ Empathetic Listening*: Strive to understand the emotions behind the words. Use empathetic phrases like, "It sounds like you feel . . ." to demonstrate your understanding and encourage deeper sharing.

4. *Utilize the Power of Silence*: Don't rush to fill pauses with your thoughts or solutions. Silence is a potent tool for both the speaker and the listener, allowing time for reflection and deeper understanding.

5. *Practice Reflective Listening*: Paraphrase and summarize what you've heard to confirm understanding. This not only demonstrates that you are listening but also helps clarify the message for both parties.

6. *Engage Your Curiosity with Questions*: Ask open-ended questions that encourage the speaker to elaborate. This signals your interest and prompts deeper insights.

7. *Cultivate Patience and Focus*: Active listening is not a passive activity. It requires energy and attention. Practice mindfulness and patience to stay engaged over longer conversations.

8. *Reflect and Act on Feedback*: After listening, reflect on what you've learned and how it affects your perspective. Implementing feedback or insights shows that you value the interaction and are committed to growth.

Mastering the art of active listening has a ripple effect far beyond the immediate conversation. It enhances relationships, fosters empathy, and promotes a culture of understanding and respect. In a world often divided by differences, active listening is a bridge to deeper connection and mutual respect.

> In a world often divided by differences, active listening is a bridge to deeper connection and mutual respect.

As you can see by now, at the heart of NeuroCoaching lies the art of crafting insightful questions and the skill of empathetic, active listening tools that are paramount in unlocking the deepest potential within individuals. These two tools alone can have a profound impact on your coaching climate and create an environment conducive to growth, learning, and understanding. Great questions, when delivered from a place of genuine curiosity and empathy, can encourage self-reflection and discovery, while active listening establishes a foundation of trust and connection. These practices not only facilitate a deeper engagement with others but also underscore the essence of effective coaching: empowering individuals to explore their thoughts and emotions, thus paving the way for meaningful change and development, which ultimately leads to higher engagement and higher performance.

Top NeuroCoaching Takeaways

1. **The power of insightful questions will amplify effective leadership and coaching.**

   We've discussed how thoughtful, well-crafted questions can unlock deeper levels of engagement in past chapters. But the neuroscience behind this process highlights how these questions stimulate dopamine (reward), oxytocin (trust), and lower cortisol (stress), depicting the science behind better communication and problem-solving.

2. **Emotional safety unlocks curiosity and growth.**

   Just as Priya's questions shifted from survival-based to exploratory as she felt more secure, the same applies to leadership and coaching. When individuals feel psychologically safe, they become more open to new ideas, feedback, and growth.

3. **Strive to maintain balance between open-ended and closed-ended questions.**

   Open-ended questions drive deeper thought and problem-solving, whereas closed-ended questions provide clarity and efficiency. The effectiveness of a conversation depends on a thoughtful balance of these question types, ensuring that engagement and understanding remain at the forefront rather than stress or defensiveness.

4. **Recognize the role of active listening in building trust and connection.**

   Active listening triggers neurological responses that can foster trust, deepen relationships, and create meaningful dialogue. Leaders who practice reflective listening and ask empathetic follow-up questions can build stronger connections and drive more impactful coaching conversations.

5. **Understand the neuroscience of questioning and learning.**

   Asking insightful questions triggers the process of instinctive elaboration, where the brain redirects its focus toward answering the question, forming new connections, and enhancing memory retention, thus encouraging individuals to see their abilities as expandable through effort and reflection.

CHAPTER 12

COACHING CLIMATE AMPLIFIER: TEAM-BASED PSYCHOLOGICAL SAFETY

Trust is built in small moments, and psychological safety is the foundation of great coaching relationships.
—Marshall Goldsmith

I REMEMBER WALKING into our high school gymnasium in May of 1986. I was asked to sing at the graduation ceremony, which was a huge thrill. It was an amazing day with my classmates as we were soon to leave our high school days behind us. What wasn't expected was the mural that spanned from floor to ceiling. If you think back to 1986, you likely remember exactly where you were for the historical shuttle launch. I'm sure some of you weren't even born yet, but if you do a Google search to 1986, it won't take you long to find a picture of the space shuttle *Challenger*.

The space shuttle *Challenger* disaster on January 28, 1986, stands as one of the most tragic events in the history of space exploration. This disaster claimed the lives of all seven crew members aboard and marked a significant moment of reflection and change for NASA and the world's approach to space travel.[1] *Challenger*, NASA's second space shuttle orbiter, was on its tenth mission, designated STS-51-L. The crew consisted of five NASA astronauts and two payload specialists, including Francis R. Scobee, the mission commander; Michael J. Smith, the pilot; Ronald McNair, Ellison Onizuka, and Judith Resnik, all mission specialists; Gregory Jarvis, a payload specialist; and *Christa McAuliffe, a high school teacher from New Hampshire*, who was selected for the Teacher in Space Project. The mural in the gymnasium was hung to honor Christa and the other astronauts who lost their lives that cold January morning.

The mission had garnered significant public interest, largely due to McAuliffe's participation, which was intended to inspire students and symbolize the accessibility of space exploration to ordinary citizens. Scheduled to launch from Kennedy Space Center in Florida, the mission aimed to conduct various experiments in orbit and deploy a satellite. In fact, the mission was "to launch the second Tracking and Data Relay System (TDRS) satellite into orbit, part of a network of satellites in geostationary Earth's orbit that, once completed, allowed near-continuous communications during shuttle missions."[2] As a communication and coaching book, I find that fact fascinating—what if we had continuous communication in our conversations with the people we most care about? Our organizations and world might be a better place.

Back to the *Challenger*.

The mission faced several delays due to weather and technical issues.[3] The final launch attempt on January 28 was conducted amidst unusually cold temperatures, a condition that would play a critical role in the ensuing disaster. Engineers at Morton Thiokol, the contractor responsible for the shuttle's solid rocket boosters, had expressed concerns about the cold temperature's effect on the O-rings, which sealed the joints of the booster segments. These concerns were not adequately addressed or communicated to decision-makers, leading to the decision to proceed with the launch.

Seventy-three seconds into the flight, *Challenger* broke apart over the Atlantic Ocean. An O-ring failure in the right solid rocket booster triggered a chain of events leading to the structural disintegration of the external fuel tank and the breakup of the orbiter.[4] The crew compartment ascended to an altitude of 65,000 feet before freefalling into the ocean. The disaster was broadcast live on television, leading to national and global shock.

President Ronald Reagan formed the Rogers Commission to investigate the accident. The commission's report, released in June 1986, concluded that the disaster was caused by the failure of the O-ring seal due to cold temperatures. It also highlighted serious flaws in NASA's decision-making process and organizational culture. The report found "a stunning lack of communication—almost as if officials had been playing a game of broken telephone, with the result that incomplete and misleading information reached NASA's top echelons."[5] Ultimately, the *Challenger* disaster was a failure in communication.

Consequently, NASA initiated major organizational and technical reforms, including redesigning the space shuttle's solid rocket boosters and implementing more stringent safety protocols. The space shuttle fleet was grounded for nearly three years following the disaster.

Challenger's tragedy profoundly impacted public perception of space exploration, emphasizing its inherent risks. It also led to a reevaluation of the balance between scientific ambition and the safety of astronauts. The disaster remains a striking reminder of the sacrifices made in the pursuit of space exploration and the importance of rigorous safety standards in any such endeavor. It's also been reported that one phone call is all it would have taken to prevent the accident; however, on that fatal day, no one made it, and the result was catastrophic.[6] How many phone calls, text messages, or conversations don't occur because our team members fear providing information to leaders? What if the culture at NASA had encouraged open conversations without fear of retribution?

The Power of Psychological Safety

Looking at *Challenger* illuminates the power of *psychological safety*. But what is psychological safety exactly, and how does it serve as an amplifier or dampener of the coaching climate?

If you go back to 1999, when Amy Edmondson, now from Harvard, published her article on psychological safety,[7] these terms weren't in the vernacular of business. I bet some of you still might find this a soft topic or a "nice to have" versus a "must have" in both individual and team environments. Led by Amy, we now have almost twenty-five years of research, and it's time for us to understand and acknowledge the impact of this work. In her latest book, *The Fearless Organization*, Amy defines psychological safety as the following:

"A climate in which people are comfortable expressing and being themselves. More specifically, when people feel psychologically safe at work, they feel comfortable sharing concerns and mistakes without fear of embarrassment or retribution."[8]

You might be wondering if psychological safety can be measured. The answer is yes. Dr. Edmondson developed The Fearless Organization Scan, which is a seven-question survey. I recommend that you look at the following questions and reflect on how your team might answer them. The questions are on a five-point Likert scale from "strongly disagree" to "strongly agree." The R represents "reverse coded," which involves reversing the scores assigned to each response. The highest score corresponds to the most negative response, and the lowest score corresponds to the most positive.

1. If I make a mistake on this team, it is often held against me [R].
2. Members of this team are able to bring up problems and tough issues.
3. People on this team sometimes reject others for being different [R].
4. It is safe to take risks on this team.
5. It is difficult to ask other members of this team for help [R].
6. No one on this team would deliberately act in a way that undermines my efforts.
7. Working with members of this team, my unique skills and talents are valued and utilized.

Let's revisit the *Challenger* tragedy. Do you think there was a fear of making a mistake? Do you believe that members of the team were fearful of bringing up problems? Do you think there was a fear of asking others for help? In this case, time was money, and there was a lot at stake! I encourage you to really look at these questions and reflect on the environment in your organization.

Tim Clark's book *The Four Stages of Psychological Safety* shares that "people flourish when they're participating in a cooperative system with high psychological safety."[9] In his book, Tim has a diagram where the bottom of the graphic is an inclusion threshold that sits between exclusion and *inclusion safety* as step one. Inclusion safety leads to *learner safety* (step two), which leads to *contributor safety* and, ultimately, *challenger safety*. In Tim's work, he references that the innovation threshold sits between contributor safety and challenger safety.[10]

In a *New York Times* article, researchers reported that good teams share two things in common. The first was that "members spoke in roughly the same proportion, a phenomenon referred to as equality in distribution of conversational turn-taking." The second was that "the teams were skilled at intuiting how others felt based on their tone of voice, their expressions, and other nonverbal cues." The article references Dr. Edmondson by quoting, "It describes a team climate characterized by interpersonal trust and mutual respect in which people are comfortable being themselves."[11]

In the Google two-year study of 180 teams, the company embarked on an initiative code-named Project Aristotle.[12] In this multi-year study, Google was searching for why some teams stumbled and others soared. It might not surprise you that they found dependability (getting things done on time and meeting a high bar of excellence), structure and clarity (clear roles, plans, and goals), meaning (work is personally important to team members), and impact (work matters and creates change) made the list. Many of these concepts align with what we have been describing in this book. The number one factor, however, was psychological safety, where team members felt safe to take risks and be vulnerable in front of each other! We must activate this in our organizations.

Coaching Tip to Activate

Psychological safety is a crucial element in fostering a productive, innovative, and positive environmental climate, whether in professional settings or personal relationships. Isaac Lidsky's story in his book *Eyes Wide Open* provides a compelling example of how this concept can be applied effectively.[13] Isaac was a childhood star in the series *Saved by the Bell: The New Class*. He was cast as the part of Weasel and was even a guest on Jeff Bloomfield's *Driving Change* podcast.[14] After listening to Isaac and reading his book, it wasn't his journey of being a star or a Harvard graduate at age nineteen or his Harvard Law degree or his experience as a law clerk for Sandra Day O'Connor and Ruth Bader Ginsburg that caught my attention. As a professor, it wasn't even his experience as a successful entrepreneur. It was his story about being a blind CEO when he realized his lack of eyesight wasn't a handicap but a superpower.

Isaac lost his sight due to a rare genetic disease, where he faced immense challenges and uncertainties. However, he turned these into opportunities for growth and success. His journey exemplifies the essence of psychological safety. He describes a story of sitting around the boardroom table, and his team was about to make a big decision. Before making the decision, he asked for his team's thoughts. As he heard nothing coming from the table, he reminded his team that he was blind and that if they had a perspective, they were going to have to talk. By giving permission and listening, each team member went around the table and contributed. After hearing from the team and considering others' input, the team made a better decision. Isaac was creating a psychologically safe environment. This then became common practice in his companies, making the teams more invested in decisions, and success followed.

To cultivate psychological safety, Isaac embraced vulnerability by admitting that not one person would have all the answers, thus creating an environment where others felt safe to do the same. He fostered open communication, encouraging team members to voice their thoughts and concerns without fear of reprisal or ridicule. This included actively listening and responding constructively to feedback. He promoted a learning culture, which shifts the blame culture to a growth and improvement culture. He led by example and encouraged deeper perspectives. Valuing diverse perspectives in a team can lead to more innovative solutions and a better understanding of challenges. If you think about this tip, it just may open the skies of your work culture and allow psychological safety to be a powerful climate amplifier.

> Valuing diverse perspectives in a team can lead to more innovative solutions and a better understanding of challenges.

By incorporating these principles, teams can create a psychologically safe environment where members feel valued, respected, and empowered to contribute their best work, leading to better outcomes and a more positive work culture.

Our offices are plastered with OSHA guidelines for physical safety. How about we leader/coaches amplify the concept of psychological safety? The time to activate is now.

Exercise to Activate

In team meetings, provide your team with the space to share their feedback before you decide on the direction to go. Require that each team member shares whether they agree, disagree, or are neutral to the decision. The team member must also provide a reason for their answer. If you wonder about the psychological safety within the team, then be transparent about why you are doing the exercise and inform them that you intend to do this consistently on team decisions. It is also important to let the team know that there are some decisions that may need to be executed if the organization has already chosen a direction. In this exercise, every team member must be given a voice. If someone has been invited to the meeting, then we will presume that was intentional.

If the team doesn't feel safe enough to share, have each individual anonymously write down their feedback. After you receive the feedback, then share the information and open the room for dialogue. I recommend you set a time for a discussion and then move to a solution. Allow this exercise to expand the opportunity for team members to speak up while also paying close attention to their nonverbal communication skills so that you intentionally build a climate that amplifies the power of voice and collaboration.

Psychological safety is the foundation of a thriving coaching climate. But how do we move beyond theory and put it into action? That's where a structured coaching climate comes in.

Top NeuroCoaching Takeaways

1. **Poor communication undermines psychological safety.**

    The breakdown in communication during the *Challenger* disaster, coupled with a high-pressure environment that discouraged speaking up, ultimately led to catastrophe. The incident, unfortunately, underscores the importance of fostering a culture where employees feel safe to voice concerns without fear of retribution.

2. **Psychological safety is key to effective teams and organizational success.**

    When employees feel safe to take risks, share ideas, and admit mistakes without fear of embarrassment or punishment, organizations see increased collaboration, innovation, and engagement. Psychological safety allows teams to move beyond surface-level conversations to deeper discussions that lead to better decision-making and problem-solving.

3. **Leadership must take active steps to cultivate psychological safety.**

    As we've discussed, leaders play a crucial role in creating an environment where team members feel valued and heard. Simple actions like ensuring everyone's voices are heard in meetings, providing a structured way for employees to share input, and leading with vulnerability can foster trust and inclusion. Organizations should prioritize psychological safety as much as they do physical safety, making it a core part of their leadership and coaching strategies.

CHAPTER 13

COACHING CLIMATE AMPLIFIER: ORGANIZATIONAL AWARENESS (POWER/POLITICS/INFLUENCE)

The key to successful leadership today is influence, not authority.
—Ken Blanchard

BOB CHAPMAN NEVER intended to become a CEO. His journey began in the 1970s when he took over the leadership of Barry-Wehmiller, a struggling manufacturing company. Back then, Chapman adhered to the traditional command-and-control style of management. He was focused on metrics, efficiency, and cost-cutting, believing that his role was to drive performance at any cost. This approach, however, created a culture of fear and low morale. Employees felt like mere cogs in a machine, and the company was mired in politics and power struggles.

But everything changed for Chapman in the early 2000s. Two pivotal moments triggered a profound transformation in his leadership philosophy.

The first came at a wedding. Chapman was a guest, watching the father of the bride give a heartfelt speech about his daughter. The father spoke with such love and pride, and Chapman was struck by a powerful realization: Every one of his employees was someone's precious child. He began to see them not as resources to be managed but as people to be cared for. Around the same time, Chapman read a book that emphasized the importance of human connections in business. This book reinforced his newfound perspective, urging him to look beyond the cold, hard metrics and see the individuals behind the numbers.

Determined to change, Chapman began to implement a radically different approach to leadership. He started with himself, embracing vulnerability and openly communicating with his employees about the company's challenges and his own uncertainties. He encouraged leaders at all levels to do the same, fostering an environment of trust and openness.

Chapman coined the term "truly human leadership" to describe his new philosophy.[1] This wasn't just about listening to employees; it was about truly understanding their needs, making them feel valued, and caring for them as individuals. He introduced leadership training programs that emphasized empathy and communication, ensuring every leader in the company embodied these values. One of Chapman's most impactful initiatives was implementing employee recognition programs. He believed every person's work should be acknowledged and celebrated. This simple act of recognition transformed the atmosphere within Barry-Wehmiller, creating a culture where employees felt appreciated and motivated.

Chapman also prioritized work-life balance and personal development, recognizing that employees who felt supported in their personal lives were more engaged and productive at work. He introduced policies that allowed for greater flexibility and opportunities for growth, ensuring that Barry-Wehmiller was not just a place of work but a community that nurtured its members.

The results of Chapman's transformation were nothing short of remarkable. Barry-Wehmiller grew from a struggling manufacturer into a thriving global enterprise. Employee engagement and morale soared, leading to increased productivity, innovation, and profitability. The company developed a reputation for its exceptional culture, attracting top talent and loyal customers.

Bob Chapman's journey is a powerful testament to the impact of leadership vulnerability and the importance of prioritizing people over politics and power. By embracing his own vulnerabilities and shifting his focus to empathy and human connection, Chapman was able to transform Barry-Wehmiller's culture and create a world-class organization. His story illustrates that true leadership is about caring for people, fostering trust, and building a supportive environment where everyone can thrive.

In any organization, understanding the dynamics of power, politics, and influence is crucial for effective coaching and leadership. These elements shape the environment in which decisions are made and actions are taken. As leaders, we must be aware of these dynamics and learn how to navigate them skillfully to foster a positive and productive coaching climate. This chapter will explore how these concepts play out across the organization and how to leverage the skills taught throughout this book to become a more aware and effective communicator when dealing with other leaders and the inevitable politics and positioning that can arise.

The Nature of Power and Influence

In any organization, power is derived from various sources, each playing a crucial role in shaping dynamics and relationships. Understanding these sources is essential for effectively navigating and influencing within an organization.

Positional Power

Imagine a manager at the top of the organizational hierarchy. Their power stems from their formal title and authority. While they can enforce rules and expect compliance due to their position, this type of power doesn't always foster genuine commitment or enthusiasm among employees.

Expert Power

Then there's the specialist, the go-to person for technical issues and complex problems. Their influence comes from their deep knowledge and expertise. Colleagues and leaders alike seek their insights, valuing their ability to solve problems and provide direction in their areas of expertise.

Relational Power

Consider the team member who seems to know everyone and has built strong, trust-based relationships throughout the company. Their influence doesn't come from their title but from the respect and trust they've earned. People naturally follow and support them because they feel understood and valued.

Personal Power

Finally, consider a charismatic leader whose presence inspires and motivates others. This person's power is rooted in their personal attributes: excellent communication skills, emotional intelligence, and the ability to connect with people on a personal level. Their influence is not about formal authority but about how they interact and engage with those around them.

Understanding these different types of power—positional, expert, relational, and personal—helps in recognizing how to navigate and influence organizational dynamics effectively. Each type plays a unique role, and the most effective leaders often leverage a combination of these sources to inspire, motivate, and guide their teams.

Stories from the Frontlines

In any organization, organizational politics is an inevitable reality. While it often carries a negative connotation, understanding and navigating it effectively is crucial for leadership. Here's a more narrative-driven look at how to approach organizational politics, illustrated through real-world examples that follow a traditional story arc.

Building a Broad Network

Sarah was a mid-level manager at a large corporation responsible for overseeing product development. Despite her ambition and skills, she found her projects frequently stalled due to a lack of support from other departments. Sarah's frustration grew as she realized that staying within her department's confines wasn't enough to push her initiatives forward.

Determined to find a solution, Sarah decided to break out of her silo. She began attending cross-departmental meetings and volunteered for interdepartmental projects. Sarah made it a point to get to know people from different areas over lunch or coffee, learning about their challenges and perspectives. Her genuine interest and efforts paid off.

As her network grew, so did the support for her projects. She found allies who championed her ideas and provided critical resources. The collaboration led to successful product launches, and Sarah's reputation as a connector and leader flourished. Her story demonstrates the power of building a broad network to navigate organizational politics effectively.

Understanding the Informal Structure

David, a project leader tasked with implementing a new company-wide software system, quickly realized that the formal hierarchy didn't always reflect how decisions were made. He struggled to gain traction with his project despite having the backing of his direct supervisors.

Frustrated but observant, David noticed that certain long-tenured employees and respected peers held significant influence over decisions, even without formal titles. He started building relationships with these key influencers, seeking their input and addressing their concerns. David's efforts to understand and navigate the informal structure paid off.

With the support of these informal leaders, David's project gained momentum. He successfully implemented the new software system, earning praise from both his supervisors and colleagues. David's journey highlights the importance of recognizing and leveraging the informal structure within an organization.

Staying Authentic

Lisa, a senior manager in the finance department, was known for her unwavering honesty and transparency. However, she found herself in a complex political situation when a critical budget decision was met with resistance from another department. Despite the pressure to compromise her values, Lisa remained true to herself. She openly communicated the rationale behind the budget decision, addressing concerns with candor and empathy. Her colleagues, initially skeptical, began to appreciate her sincerity and straightforwardness.

Over time, Lisa's authenticity built a strong foundation of trust. Her department's decisions were respected, and she became a go-to leader for advice and collaboration. Lisa's story illustrates how staying authentic, even in politically charged situations, can enhance influence and build lasting relationships.

Advocating for Transparency

John, a department head in the human resources division, knew that opacity in decision-making bred mistrust and resentment. Facing a significant organizational change, he decided to promote transparency by openly discussing decisions and involving his team in the process. He held regular town halls where employees could ask questions and voice concerns. Initially, the atmosphere was tense, with employees wary of the changes. However, John's consistent efforts to be open and transparent gradually eased tensions. Employees began to feel heard and valued, contributing their ideas and feedback.

This practice not only fostered a culture of openness but also minimized the negative aspects of organizational politics. John's commitment to transparency transformed his department, making it a model for others in the company. His story underscores the benefits of advocating for transparency in navigating organizational politics.

Building Alliances

Emma, a product manager in the R&D department of a tech company, was passionate about innovation. She had brilliant ideas for new products, but she struggled to get her proposals approved by senior management. Despite her expertise, Emma found that her projects often faced resistance, especially from departments that were wary of change.

One day, Emma decided to change her approach. Instead of working in isolation, she began to focus on building alliances within the company. She took the time to understand the interests and motivations of key stakeholders, from the finance team concerned about budgets to the marketing department focused on customer needs. Emma started small, collaborating on a few projects that aligned with the goals of these departments. She actively sought their input, making them feel involved and valued.

Emma's breakthrough came when she proposed a new software product. Instead of presenting it as a stand-alone R&D project, she framed it as a collaborative effort that addressed the needs of multiple departments. She demonstrated how the new product would drive sales, streamline operations, and enhance customer satisfaction. Her approach won the support of key influencers who had previously been skeptical.

With their backing, Emma's project gained momentum. The collaborative environment she fostered led to successful product development and a well-received market launch. Her ability to build alliances turned her into a respected leader and innovator within the company. Emma's journey underscores the importance of understanding and aligning with others' goals to navigate organizational politics effectively.

Managing Conflicts

Alex, a senior engineer at an automotive company, was often caught in the middle of conflicts between different departments. One particularly challenging situation arose during the development of a new car model. The engineering team wanted to incorporate cutting-edge technology, while the sales team pushed for features that would appeal to a broader market. The disagreement escalated, causing delays and tension.

Alex decided to step in and mediate. He organized a series of meetings where each side could voice their concerns and aspirations. In the first meeting, he encouraged the engineering team to explain the benefits of the new technology, emphasizing how it could set their car apart from competitors. In the next meeting, he facilitated a discussion with the sales team, highlighting the importance of market appeal and customer preferences.

As the conversations progressed, Alex used active listening to understand the underlying issues. He realized that both teams had valid points but were viewing the project from different perspectives. By acknowledging each side's contributions and finding common ground, Alex proposed a compromise: incorporating some of the advanced technology while ensuring the car retained features that appealed to a broad market segment.

This collaborative approach not only resolved the conflict but also strengthened interdepartmental relationships. The final product was a success, praised for its innovative features and market appeal. Alex's story demonstrates the power of constructive conflict management in navigating organizational politics and fostering a collaborative culture.

Communicating Effectively

Jessica, the communications director at a healthcare organization, was known for her ability to articulate complex ideas clearly. Her role often required her to present new initiatives to both the executive team and frontline staff, a challenge given the diverse audiences.

When tasked with introducing a new patient care system, Jessica knew she had to gain buy-in from both groups. For the executives, she prepared a detailed presentation, emphasizing the system's potential to improve patient outcomes and reduce costs. She used data and projections to support her points, addressing their strategic concerns.

However, when presenting to the frontline staff, Jessica took a different approach. She held informal meetings and used storytelling to convey the benefits of the new system. She shared real-life scenarios demonstrating how the system would make their jobs easier and improve patient care. Jessica listened to their concerns and provided practical answers, making them feel involved and valued.

Jessica's dual approach paid off. Executives approved the initiative, seeing its strategic value, while the frontline staff embraced the change, understanding its practical benefits. Her ability to adapt her communication style to different audiences ensured a smooth implementation of the new system. Jessica's story highlights the importance of effective communication in navigating organizational politics and achieving organizational goals.

Leveraging Neuroscience Principles: Emotional Intelligence (EI)

Tom, a sales leader at a financial services firm, was known for his high emotional intelligence. He understood that his success depended not just on his technical skills but also on his ability to connect with people. One of his biggest challenges was managing a high-performing but volatile sales team. Tom noticed that one of his top performers, Rachel, often had emotional outbursts when deals didn't go as planned. Instead of reprimanding her, Tom decided to leverage his emotional intelligence. He scheduled a one-on-one meeting with Rachel, where he practiced active listening. Rachel shared her frustrations about the high pressure and her fear of failure.

By understanding Rachel's emotional triggers, Tom helped her develop better coping strategies. He introduced stress management techniques and provided her with resources to improve her resilience. Tom also adjusted his management style, offering more support and recognition to boost her confidence. Over time, Rachel's performance improved, and her emotional stability enhanced team morale. Tom's empathetic approach not only retained a valuable team member but also strengthened the overall team dynamics. His story illustrates how developing and leveraging emotional intelligence can effectively navigate organizational politics and enhance leadership.

Building Trust

Mia, a manufacturing company operations manager, believed that trust was the cornerstone of effective leadership. However, she inherited a team that was skeptical and disengaged due to past leadership failures. Mia knew she had to rebuild trust from the ground up.

She started by being consistently transparent and honest in her communications. Mia held regular team meetings where she openly discussed the challenges and progress of their projects. She also made herself available for individual meetings, where team members could express their concerns and suggestions. One significant turning point came when Mia admitted to a mistake she had made in project planning. Instead of deflecting blame, she took full responsibility and shared her plan to rectify the issue. Her vulnerability and accountability resonated with her team, who began to see her as a trustworthy and reliable leader.

Mia also fostered a culture of mutual respect by recognizing and celebrating her team's achievements. She used elements from the "Periodic Table of Trust," such as vulnerability, honesty, and authenticity, to build strong relationships. Over time, the team's performance improved, and their engagement levels soared. Mia's journey highlights the critical role of trust in navigating organizational politics and leading effectively.

Activating the Right Brain Networks

Kevin, the chief strategist at a global consulting firm, understood the importance of balancing analytical and empathic thinking. He faced a major challenge when the firm decided to undergo a significant restructuring to stay competitive. The decision was met with anxiety and resistance from employees at all levels. Kevin knew that relying solely on data and logic wouldn't be enough to win hearts and minds. He used the analytical network (AN) to develop a clear, data-driven rationale for the restructuring, emphasizing the strategic benefits and long-term growth prospects. He presented these findings to the executive team, securing their buy-in.

Simultaneously, Kevin engaged the empathic network (EN) to address employees' emotional concerns. He held town hall meetings and small group discussions where he listened to their fears and frustrations. Kevin shared stories about other companies that had successfully navigated similar changes, providing reassurance and hope.

By balancing both networks, Kevin created a comprehensive approach that addressed both the logical and emotional aspects of the restructuring. The transition was smoother than expected, with employees feeling more understood and valued. Kevin's story demonstrates how activating the right brain networks can help navigate complex organizational changes effectively.

Practical Strategies for Leaders

Navigating organizational politics can be a complex yet essential part of leadership. Success often hinges not just on what you know, but on how well you understand power dynamics, navigate relationships, and communicate with influence. The following stories of Samantha, James, and Laura offer examples of how leaders can build political acumen by conducting power audits, developing political savvy, and enhancing communication skills to drive change and build alignment.

Conducting Power Audits

Samantha, a director of corporate strategy at a multinational corporation, faced a challenging task: She needed to implement a new strategic initiative across diverse regions with varying power dynamics. To navigate this, she conducted regular power audits to assess the influence and impact of key players within the organization. Samantha identified not only formal leaders but also informal influencers who had significant sway over their colleagues. She mapped out the power dynamics, understanding who could serve as potential allies or adversaries. This awareness allowed her to tailor her approach when introducing the new initiative.

By engaging these key influencers early and incorporating their feedback, Samantha built a coalition of support. The initiative gained traction, and she successfully navigated the complex power structures within the organization. Her story illustrates the importance of conducting power audits to understand and leverage organizational dynamics.

Developing Political Savvy

James, a business development manager at a fast-growing tech startup, quickly realized that staying informed about organizational changes and developments was crucial. He anticipated the political implications of his actions and decisions, developing a keen sense of political savvy. James built a reputation for being well-informed and strategically minded. He networked with colleagues across the company, gaining insights into their priorities and concerns. When a major merger was announced, James used his political acumen to navigate the ensuing uncertainty.

He aligned himself with key decision-makers and demonstrated how his projects could support the merger's goals. His proactive approach earned him a seat at the table, where he could influence the direction of the merger's implementation. James's story highlights the value of political savvy in advancing organizational goals.

Enhancing Communication Skills

Laura, a customer service leader at a retail company, was known for her exceptional communication skills. She faced a major challenge when the company decided to overhaul its customer service processes. The change was met with skepticism and resistance from the frontline staff. Laura practiced active listening and asked open-ended questions to understand their concerns. She used positive language and framing to highlight the benefits of the new processes, emphasizing how they would improve both employee experience and customer satisfaction. Laura was also mindful of her nonverbal communication cues, ensuring her body language matched her words. Her approach built trust and buy-in from the staff, leading to a successful implementation of the new processes. Laura's story underscores the importance of enhancing communication skills to navigate organizational politics and drive change.

By embracing these strategies and understanding the nature of power and influence, leaders can effectively navigate organizational politics, fostering a culture of trust, transparency, and collaboration.

Top NeuroCoaching Takeaways

1. **Recognize the power of human-centered leadership.**

    Bob Chapman's leadership transformation illustrates the profound impact of shifting from a command-and-control mindset to a people-first approach. By recognizing employees as individuals with personal value—rather than just workers—he cultivated an environment of trust, engagement, and higher performance.

2. **Different forms of power can influence organizational dynamics.**

    The power within organizations comes in multiple forms, including positional power (formal authority), expert power (knowledge and skills), relational power (trust-based influence), and personal power (charisma and emotional intelligence). Effective leaders recognize and leverage these to navigate complex dynamics and drive positive change.

3. **Navigating organizational politics requires awareness and strategic action.**

    Politics in the workplace is inevitable, but leaders who build broad networks and foster trust can successfully navigate these challenges. Stories of leaders like Sarah, David, and Lisa illustrate the importance of relationship-building, staying authentic, and advocating for transparency in decision-making to create an inclusive and collaborative work culture.

4. **Emotional intelligence and active listening strengthen leadership impact.**

    The ability to connect with others through emotional intelligence (EI) is crucial for effective leadership. Leaders who recognize emotional triggers and respond with empathy can improve team morale, resolve conflicts, and foster a culture of support and collaboration.

5. **Strategic communication and influence drive organizational success.**

    Whether it's tailoring messages to different audiences, balancing data-driven logic with emotional connection, or leveraging key influencers within an organization, strong communication skills play a vital role in leadership success. Stories of leaders like Jessica and Kevin highlight how balancing analytical and empathic approaches creates stronger engagement and smoother transitions during organizational changes.

CHAPTER 14

COACHING CLIMATE AMPLIFIERS: THE IMPACT OF VR/AR AND AI ON COACHING

There will be two kinds of companies in the future: those that are great at AI and everybody else.

—Mark Cuban

PICTURE THIS: YOU'RE standing at the edge of the Grand Canyon, your heart racing as you look down at the vast expanse below. But here's the twist—you're not actually there. You're in a virtual reality environment, and a calm voice in your headset is guiding you through a breathing exercise. This isn't just a cool tech demo; it's a coaching session designed to help you overcome fear using cutting-edge principles from neuroscience and psychology.

This scenario isn't just a glimpse into the future of coaching—it's happening right now. And it's not just conquering fears. Virtual reality (VR), augmented reality (AR), and artificial intelligence (AI) are revolutionizing how we approach coaching in the business world.

Traditionally, coaching has relied on face-to-face interactions, whether in person or through video calls. While these methods can be effective, they have their limitations. They often lack the immersive and interactive elements that can drive deeper behavioral change. That's where VR, AR, and AI come in, transforming not just how coaching is delivered but how it's experienced.

Let's dive into some examples of how these technologies are shaking things up.

Leadership Development Gets Real (Virtually)

Imagine you're a rising star in your company, and you're enrolled in a leadership development program. Instead of just discussing theoretical scenarios in a boardroom, you find yourself immersed in a virtual environment. You're suddenly in the hot seat, navigating high-stress situations, negotiating deals, and managing team conflicts in real time.

This isn't just a fancy way to make training more entertaining. There's solid science behind it. When you're in a VR environment, your brain activates the same neural pathways it would in real-world experiences. Your mirror neurons, which help you learn through observation, are firing on all cylinders. This means the lessons learned in this virtual boardroom can translate directly into real-world behavior.

There's also a psychological principle at play here called *embodied cognition*. It suggests that our thoughts and feelings are deeply influenced by our physical experiences. By physically (well, virtually) embodying different roles, you develop a deeper understanding and empathy—crucial skills for effective leadership and teamwork.

AI: Your Personal Performance Coach

Now, let's talk about how AI is changing the game. Imagine you are in sales manager training. As you practice a coaching scenario, an AI-powered tool analyzes your every move. It's not just listening to your words; it's picking up on your speech patterns, body language, and even your emotional cues. And the best part? You get instant feedback on how to improve. This real-time analysis and feedback are game-changers from a neuroscience perspective. You see, our brains are most receptive to change when feedback is immediate and specific. It's like training a puppy—the quicker you reinforce good behavior, the more likely it is to stick. AI's ability to provide this kind of instant, tailored feedback ensures that your learning is both efficient and impactful.

Emotional Intelligence: Practice Makes Perfect

Developing emotional intelligence and other soft skills (redefined as real skills) can be difficult. It's not like learning a new software where you can just follow a manual. This is where AI shines again. Using natural language processing and machine learning, AI can create realistic conversational agents that mimic human interactions.

Imagine practicing a difficult conversation with an AI-powered "colleague" who responds just like a real person would. You can try different approaches, receive feedback on your emotional responses, and refine your technique—all in a risk-free environment. This ties into the psychological principle of social learning, where we pick up behaviors and skills by observing and imitating others. By interacting with these AI agents, you're essentially getting a personal trainer for your social skills. You can practice, make mistakes, and learn without the fear of real-world consequences. It's like having a flight simulator for your interpersonal skills!

Revolutionizing Sales Training

Imagine you're a sales rep, and instead of role-playing with your colleagues, you're about to enter a virtual sales pitch scenario. You put on your VR headset, and suddenly, you're in a boardroom with potential clients. These aren't just static avatars—they have realistic body language and facial expressions. Your task? Navigate the sales pitch, handle objections, and close the deal in real time.

This isn't just a fancy way to make training more entertaining. There's some serious brain science at work here. When you're in this immersive VR experience, your brain's mirror neurons light up like a Christmas tree. These neurons, which fire when you observe or imagine actions, are working overtime in this virtual environment. The result? Your brain treats this practice almost like the real deal, making it incredibly effective for learning.

But wait, there's more! While you're pitching your heart out, AI algorithms are working behind the scenes. They're analyzing your speech patterns, tone, body language, and even your emotional cues. Stumble over your words or use ineffective language? The AI catches it and provides instant feedback. It's like having a personal coach whispering in your ear, helping you refine your technique in real time.

Remember how we talked about the importance of repetition in learning? This is where AI-powered coaching tools really shine. Based on your performance data, these tools can generate personalized practice sessions tailored to your specific needs. Struggle with handling objections? The AI will create scenarios that focus on that. Need to work on your closing techniques? You'll get plenty of practice there too. This personalized approach is crucial because it helps strengthen those neural pathways we talked about earlier. The more you practice these tailored exercises, the more automatic and effective your sales behaviors become over time.

One of the most fascinating things about this tech-powered training is how it can replicate the emotional intensity of real sales environments. When you're in a high-stakes VR simulation, your brain's emotional center—the amygdala—kicks into high gear. This emotional engagement makes the experience more memorable, ensuring that the techniques you practice stick with you when you're in real-world situations. And here's the kicker—this type of training is incredibly scalable. Whether you're a sales team of 5 or 5,000 spread across different continents, everyone can access the same high-quality, personalized training. It's like democratizing access to top-tier sales coaching, ensuring consistency and excellence across your entire organization.

The Neuroscience behind It All

Now, let's geek out a bit on the brain science that makes all this so effective. One of the biggest advantages of VR and AR in coaching is their ability to create highly engaging learning environments. These technologies demand your full attention and involvement, which is great news for your brain. Why? It all comes down to dopamine—often called the "feel-good" or "reward" neurotransmitter. When you're engaged in an enjoyable or rewarding task, your brain releases dopamine. This not only makes you feel good but also enhances your motivation and reinforces learning.

But dopamine isn't just about feeling good. It plays a crucial role in memory formation too. When dopamine is released, it helps your brain's memory center—the hippocampus—encode new information more effectively. This means that the skills and techniques you practice in these engaging VR sessions are more likely to stick with you long-term.

Emotions and Learning: A Powerful Combo

Here's another important aspect of VR and AR—they can create emotionally charged experiences. And when it comes to learning, emotions are like rocket fuel for your brain. When you're in an emotionally charged situation (even a virtual one), it activates your amygdala—the brain's emotional processing center. The amygdala then signals to your hippocampus, "Hey, this is important stuff! Make sure we remember this!" As a result, emotionally charged experiences are more likely to be etched into your long-term memory.

This is why the VR crisis management scenario we talked about earlier can be so effective. The stress and intensity you feel during the simulation make the lessons learned more memorable and easier to remember when you face a real crisis.

Repetition: The Key to Mastery

We've all heard the phrase "practice makes perfect," right? Well, there's solid neuroscience backing that up. Repeated practice strengthens the neural pathways associated with a particular skill or behavior, making it more automatic over time. This is where AI-powered coaching tools really shine. They can provide continuous, personalized practice opportunities, reinforcing learning through repetition. It's like having a personal trainer for your brain, helping you build those neural muscles through targeted exercises.

For example, let's say you're working on improving your public speaking skills. An AI-driven coaching platform could analyze your speeches, providing feedback on things like tone, pacing, and body language. Based on this analysis, it could then generate personalized practice sessions targeting your specific weaknesses. Over time, this continuous, targeted practice reinforces the neural pathways associated with effective public speaking, making the behavior more natural and automatic.

The Democratization of Coaching

One of the most exciting aspects of these technologies is how they're making high-quality coaching accessible to more people. AI can scale personalized coaching, providing tailored guidance to employees at all levels, regardless of where they are in the world. This democratization of coaching can lead to a more skilled and competent workforce across the board. Moreover, AI provides data-driven insights into performance, highlighting strengths and areas for improvement. This allows for more targeted coaching interventions, maximizing the impact of coaching efforts. It's like having a GPS for your professional development, showing you exactly where you need to go and how to get there.

Creating Safe Environments for Learning

Another significant advantage of VR and AR is their ability to create safe spaces for employees to practice and learn without the fear of real-world consequences. This encourages experimentation and innovation, as participants can take risks and learn from their mistakes in a controlled environment. Think about it: How many times have you held back from trying something new at work because you were afraid of messing up? With VR and AR, you can take those risks, make those mistakes, and learn from them without any real-world fallout. It's like having a playground for your professional skills, where you can experiment and grow without fear.

Challenges and Potential Drawbacks

Now, it's not all sunshine and rainbows. Like any new technology, VR, AR, and AI in coaching come with their own set of challenges and potential drawbacks.

The Human Touch

One of the biggest concerns is the risk of becoming overly reliant on technology and neglecting the human element of coaching. While AI can provide valuable insights and feedback, it can't replace the empathy, intuition, and personal connection that human coaches bring to the table. There's something to be said for the wisdom and experience of a seasoned coach that even the most advanced AI can't fully replicate—at least not yet.

Privacy and Ethical Concerns

Using AI in coaching also raises some important privacy and ethical questions. These tools collect a lot of data about individuals—their performance, behaviors, and even their emotional responses. This data needs to be handled with extreme care to protect privacy and ensure it's used ethically. We need to be vigilant about setting up proper safeguards and guidelines for the use of this technology.

The Digital Divide

While these technologies have the potential to democratize coaching, there's also a risk of creating a new kind of digital divide. Not all organizations can afford the latest VR, AR, and AI tools, which could potentially widen the gap between those with access to advanced coaching technologies and those without. We need to be mindful of this and work on making these technologies more accessible to all.

The Future of Coaching: A Brave New World

So where do we go from here? The integration of VR, AR, and AI into coaching is going to continue evolving, driven by advancements in technology and our deepening understanding of the neuroscience and psychology behind learning and development.

One trend we're likely to see is the rise of blended coaching models. These will combine human coaches with AI-powered tools and VR/AR experiences. This hybrid approach can leverage the strengths of both technology and human intuition, providing a more holistic coaching experience. Imagine having an AI assistant that provides data-driven insights to support your human coach's expertise—it's like having the best of both worlds.

We're also likely to see a shift toward continuous learning and development. AI's ability to provide ongoing, personalized feedback will drive this change. Instead of isolated training sessions, employees will have access to continuous coaching and support, fostering a culture of constant improvement and growth. It's like having a personal trainer for your career, always there to help you improve and evolve.

As AI and VR/AR technologies become more sophisticated, they'll offer even more realistic and effective training for emotional and social skills. This will be crucial for developing leaders who can navigate the complexities of modern business environments with empathy and emotional intelligence. Imagine being able to practice difficult conversations or complex negotiations in hyper-realistic virtual environments—it's a game-changer for developing these crucial soft skills.

Wrapping It Up

The impact of VR, AR, and AI on coaching in the business world is nothing short of revolutionary. These technologies are offering new opportunities to enhance learning and development in ways we could only dream of a few years ago. By leveraging the neuroscience and psychology behind these technologies, we can create coaching experiences that are not just more effective but also more engaging and impactful. But as we embrace these innovations, it's crucial to strike a balance. We need to harness the power of technology while preserving the human touch that makes coaching such a powerful tool for personal and professional development. It's about using technology to enhance, not replace, the human elements of coaching.

As we stand on the brink of this new era in coaching, the possibilities seem limitless. Just like that virtual Grand Canyon experience we started with, we're looking out at a vast expanse of potential. It's exciting, maybe a little scary, but full of opportunities for growth and development.

The future of coaching is here, and it's virtual, augmented, and artificially intelligent. Are you ready?

Top NeuroCoaching Takeaways

1. **VR, AR, and AI are revolutionizing coaching and leadership development.**

   Traditional coaching methods are being transformed by immersive technologies. These tools allow individuals to engage in realistic, high-stakes scenarios—whether it's practicing leadership, handling difficult conversations, or refining sales pitches. The neuroscience behind these technologies, such as *embodied cognition* and *mirror neurons*, ensures that experiences in virtual environments translate into real-world behavior changes.

2. **AI-powered feedback enhances learning efficiency and retention.**

   AI-driven coaching tools analyze speech patterns, body language, and emotional cues to provide immediate, data-driven feedback. By offering real-time personalized coaching, AI ensures that individuals continuously refine their skills in a way that traditional training often fails to achieve.

3. **Emotional intelligence and soft skills can be practiced in risk-free environments.**

   Developing emotional intelligence is difficult due to real-world trial and error. AI-powered simulations and virtual conversations, though, can create *safe spaces* for individuals to practice difficult discussions, conflict resolution, and interpersonal skills.

4. **Balancing technology with human connection is essential for effective coaching.**

   Don't be fooled: AI and VR can't replace empathy, intuition, and personal connections that are still needed for critical elements of effective coaching. The future of coaching will likely blend AI-driven insights with human expertise for a more comprehensive learning experience.

CHAPTER 15

CASE STUDY & COACHING THOUGHTS

A good coach can change a game. A great coach can change a life.
—John Wooden

IN TODAY'S FAST-PACED life sciences landscape, leadership requires more than technical expertise; it demands intentional, human-centered coaching. One global organization recognized the need to elevate communication and career development across its teams. Through Braintrust's NeuroCoaching and NeuroSelling programs, they equipped over 60 leaders and 300 account managers with the tools to foster a culture of world-class communicators. From high-stakes promotion conversations to building a consistent coaching cadence, the transformation has been both measurable and meaningful.

CASE STUDY: Coaching for Career Growth in Life Sciences

Industry: Life Sciences

Geography: Global

Region: North America

Partnership Length: Seeking long-term collaboration (currently multi-year)

Services Provided: NeuroCoaching® and NeuroSelling®

Training Impact: 60+ Leaders & 300 Account Managers

The Challenge

The organization faced a lack of consistency and intentionality in communication—both internally with employees and externally with customers. To address this, they set a clear mission:

> "Create a culture of world-class communicators throughout North America."

The NeuroCoaching® Leadership Development Approach

To drive performance and reinforce a "serve to solve" mindset, the organization implemented a structured coaching framework.

1. **NeuroVision™ Process**
   A proprietary approach to aligning vision at the organizational, leader, and employee levels. This phase focused on developing a people development vision to foster a strong coaching culture.

2. **Situational Conversations Skills Training**
   Live and virtual training sessions that improved leaders' ability to engage in impactful conversations.

3. **Coaching Reinforcement**
   Practice and repetition to ensure sustainable communication improvements across teams.

Key Measurement Goals

- Boost engagement, retention, and overall performance
- Strengthen motivation, loyalty, and productivity
- Enhance key performance metrics and individual growth
- Improve leadership pipeline and long-term culture-building
- Create a better workplace environment with stronger results

Client Testimonial

"NeuroCoaching™ helped my team translate neuroscience principles into a practical model that will have a lasting impact on team development and performance. We were looking for a sustainable coaching

model, and we got it. As a team, we crystallized a foundational vision for our business unit, each leader, and our employees. This program will take us from being a good company to a great leadership organization. Thanks to the Braintrust team."

Coaching Scenario: Preparing for a Promotion Opportunity

Employee's Profile:

- Serves two roles in the organization
- Highly proactive and a strong team player
- Has been with the company for over a year
- Demonstrates a commitment to excellence

Coaching Situation

The employee became aware of a manager promotion opportunity due to an upcoming expansion. He proactively approached his leader to discuss his qualifications and seek guidance on preparing for the selection process. The leader understood this wouldn't be a single conversation but an ongoing coaching journey.

Situational Conversation Road Map (The Stoplight Approach)

1. **Purpose**
    - The employee scheduled this conversation to discuss his readiness for the manager role.
    - He wanted guidance on how to approach the selection process effectively.

2. **Perspective**
   - The employee and leader had already worked on an individual development plan (IDP) to identify strengths and areas for growth.
   - Areas for improvement: driving results, increasing engagement, and developing talent.

3. **Plan/Path**

   The plan was structured around key performance indicators:
   - **Driving Results** – Consistently ranks in the top tier.
   - **Engagement Leadership** – Leads training classes for new hires.
   - **Developing Talent** – Has actively mentored newer team members:
     - Supported Joe, a new hire, through multiple product training attempts.
     - Established "office hours" for Samantha to discuss her development needs.

   Action Plan:
   - The employee would present his development journey during the interview process and demonstrate how his leadership contributions align with the organization's goals.
   - Regular coaching check-ins were planned leading up to the interviews.

   Side Note: The employee recalled a past colleague who didn't secure a similar promotion but also didn't take advantage of interview feedback—a lesson he wanted to learn from.

4. **Progress**
    - The employee's success would be measured through interview performance and feedback.
    - The leader challenged him to self-assess his progress in key areas and prepare an interview PowerPoint to highlight his strengths and experiences.

5. **Problems**
    - The employee acknowledged a gap in leadership experience that could impact his readiness for the new role.
    - He wanted to address this proactively rather than waiting for a future opportunity.

6. **Performance**
    - Success would be defined in two ways:
        - Ideal Outcome: The employee secures the promotion.
        - Alternative Outcome: If not selected, he would use feedback as a growth opportunity and refine his development plan for future leadership roles.
    - The leader and employee agreed to celebrate progress regardless of the outcome to keep motivation high.

Key Takeaways for NeuroCoaching Learners

As you reflect on this case, consider these questions:

1. Was there a clear shared vision between the leader and employee?
2. Did the leader and employee define the purpose before the conversation?
3. How well did the employee understand and prepare for different perspectives in the conversation?
4. Was there a structured plan to guide the coaching process?
5. How was progress measured and evaluated?
6. Were potential challenges and roadblocks anticipated?
7. How did the leader support the employee's long-term growth and aspirations?

This case highlights the power of intentional coaching in career development. By using the NeuroCoaching framework, the leader ensured that the employee felt supported, had a road map for success, and gained valuable self-awareness—whether he secured the promotion or not.

How would you coach in a similar scenario?

Situational Coaching Conversations – Your Turn

Scenario Play: Running the Coaching Playbook on Five Situations

Step 1: *Select a Coaching Scenario*

Think about a recent or upcoming coaching conversation. Consider:

- The person you are coaching (employee, peer, leader, friend)
- The situation you need to address
- The desired outcome of the conversation
- The actual outcome that occurred

Now, let's assume that you and the other person already have a strong shared vision and a clearly aligned mission for growth. If this foundation is weak, take a step back and reinforce it first.

Got your scenario in mind? Great. Now, let's move through the 6P's coaching road map to structure your conversation effectively.

The 6P's Framework for Situational Coaching Conversations

1. PURPOSE
What is the driving reason behind this conversation?

- Is this about growth, performance, feedback, motivation, or a strategic decision?
- What outcome are you hoping to achieve?

2. PERSPECTIVE
Whose perspective are you considering?

- Have you thought about the other person's experience, emotions, and current mindset?
- How might their perspective differ from yours?
- What biases might you need to challenge?

3. PLAN/PATH
What's the game plan for this conversation?

- Is there a clear and agreed-upon strategy to move forward?
- Are you addressing both short-term actions and long-term development?
- Are we on or off the path?
- When we think of success, should we consider another path?

The 6P's Framework for Situational Coaching Conversations

4. PROGRESS
How will success be measured?

- What specific steps will indicate growth or movement in the right direction?
- How will you follow up to ensure the plan is working?

5. PROBLEMS
What challenges might arise?

- Are there known roadblocks that could derail progress?
- Who is responsible for navigating and resolving these challenges?

6. PERFORMANCE
How will the results be reviewed and celebrated?

- What does success look like?
- How will you recognize and reinforce positive behaviors and outcomes?

Your Challenge: Run This Playbook on Five Coaching Scenarios

To truly master situational fluency in coaching, you need practice and repetition. Select at least five different scenarios and apply the 6P's Framework to each. Consider the following examples:

- A performance conversation with a direct report
- A peer coaching situation in a cross-functional project
- A development discussion with a high-potential employee
- A feedback session following a challenge or mistake
- A mentorship conversation for career growth

For each scenario, walk through the six key areas, identify gaps, and adjust your approach.

Final Thought: Breaking through the Stoplights

The 6P's Framework ensures that coaching conversations don't get stuck at red lights. When you proactively set purpose, perspective, and a plan/path, you gain momentum. When you anticipate challenges, track progress, and celebrate performance, you build trust and lasting engagement.

Now, it's time to put this into action. Choose your five scenarios and start coaching with intention.

Coaching Thoughts

A friend once told me that we shouldn't judge someone's life by just one chapter. What if someone opened your book and made all their judgments about you based solely on a few pages? As leaders and coaches, we're always under a critical focus to never stop building onto relationships, but we're still a composition of our stories and continuingly adding to them.

Think back to the beginning of the book, when I shared a tense moment with an employee. I may not have fully understood at that moment where Chris, my employee, was coming from, but Chris also didn't realize the pressure I was receiving from the senior executives. There's always more to the story when it comes to coaching.

In his book *Relational Coach*, Erik de Haan speaks to the concept that in any conversation, a coach has two main choices. The first is the *direction of their contribution*, and the second is the *nature of the contribution*.[1] This was a profound insight for me as we developed the framework you have in your hands. Erik goes on to explain that the coach decides whether they are "exploring" or "guiding" as they think about the direction of the conversation. There's a difference in how you attack these approaches. In one case, you're proposing something. In the second, you're at the service of "joint exploration or discovery." Erik explains that each moment, you are deciding to build and reinforce the "coachee's (perceived) strengths, or you assist in overcoming the coachee's (perceived) weaknesses."[2] In coaching, we are constantly making decisions to support or challenge the team members we're coaching.

Here's the question for you: Are goals important? Hopefully, you answered yes. I want you to reposition goals for the remainder of our work and time together. If you set up clear standards (aligned mission), then it's easier to co-establish goals for an individual and team at the beginning. When it comes to goals, I want you to stop coaching to the goal and start coaching to the plan/path. Goals are important, but a great plan with accountability to measure progress is even better.

> *"Stop coaching to the goal and start coaching to the plan."*

We also want our team members to understand that there aren't secrets in coaching. We recommend proactively showing your team members the framework. The more they know, the more you increase transparency.

> *"There are no secrets in coaching—be transparent."*

As a coaching point for your conversations, keep looking through the lens of your team members. As de Haan states in *Relational Coaching*, the aim of coaching is to improve the coachees' performance by discussing their relationship to certain experiences and issues.[3]

> *"The coach's intention is to encourage reflection by the coachee, to release hidden strengths and to overcome or eliminate obstacles to further development."*[4]

All of our team members are on a journey, and it's our job to help guide them to performance regardless of where they are on the path. There's always more to every story. I hope you can clearly see the connection of this type of philosophy with our approach to neuroscience and our framework, that relational coaching opens our employees to new ideas and perspectives.

Case Study & Coaching Thoughts

> *"When the coach feels relatively secure
> in relation to many of their own tensions and anxieties,
> they can focus genuinely on the coachee and the coachee's issues
> and what concerns the coachee has at this specific moment.
> This is a unique combination of thin and thick skin,
> a balance between open-mindedness, tension, and certainty.
> A balance that is constantly changing and hence adjusting."[5]*

This can help your coachees to think divergently about problem-solving and decision-making. It also allows you, as the coach, to be more transactional when needed. The best coaches know how to balance both relational and transactional elements of coaching; they can dial them up and down in different situational scenarios. There's no doubt that context matters. It's no different than a great musician who can only play one chord. The chord might be perfect, but it doesn't make a great song.

In therapy literature, there're published commandments from intervention to interaction based on the effectiveness of therapy. As you process your coaching journey, take a moment and reflect on this list to see if you overlap with our coaching framework. I hope you do.

1. First, do no harm.
2. Have confidence.
3. Commit your heart and soul to your approach.
4. Feed the hope of your coachee.
5. Consider the coaching situation from your coachees' perspective.
6. Work on your coaching relationship.
7. If you don't click, find a replacement coach.
8. Look after yourself to keep yourself as healthy as possible.
9. Try to stay fresh and unbiased.
10. Don't worry too much about the specific things you are doing.

A Leadership Perspective: Coach Nick Saban

Shifting gears to another form of coaching, athletic coaching, I can't think of a better example than coach Nick Saban, head coach of the University of Alabama football team. I view him in a similar light to Coach Debo Sweeney (Clemson University), Former Coach Mike Krzyzewski "Coach K" (Duke University), or the late great Pat Summitt (University of Tennessee). Coach Saban has had seven national championships, including one at LSU and six at Alabama (2009, 2011, 2012, 2015, 2017 & 2020). However, his success isn't what caught my attention, but rather his philosophy on coaching, his perspective on players, and his coaching rehab program. In an article published about him in 2021 titled "Inside Nick Saban's Coaching Rehab: Resurrecting Careers at Alabama, One Sullied Coach at a Time," the subtitle states that coaches are "joining the Crimson Tide as damaged goods and coming out clean with big opportunities on the other side."[6] Coach Saban focuses on a windshield approach to coaching (looking forward) rather than dwelling on the rearview approach (looking back) or perhaps a few pages of someone's story. Saban stated the following:

"We're always looking for a better way. Those guys, all good coaches, all did a really good job somewhere along the line before. I'm sure they had their own ambitions of what they wanted to accomplish and what they wanted to do here, whether it was to overcome previous failings or learn from people here."

The article goes on to describe over three decades of what Saban calls his "coaching tree" and how difficult it is to hire people. He says at the end of the day:

"People make the organization what it is."

In the pursuit of victory, both on the field and in the greater game of life, one's mindset is undoubtedly the tipping point for success. Coach Saban seems to exemplify this with his team, players, coaches, and university. By forging a path to high performance, Saban states that one must first conjure a clear and unwavering vision of what they aspire to achieve. But this vision isn't a mere desire for success within the game; it extends further into the realm of life and the true impact of one's journey. His program manifests as a higher probability of prosperity in all endeavors.

The blueprint for reaching this vision lies in a meticulously defined process—a road map carved with the precision of discipline.

> *"Discipline is the unyielding commitment to undertake tasks that are necessary yet often undesirable. It is the choice to engage in the actions that propel one toward the crystallization of their vision."*

In a powerful motivational video of Coach Saban, he describes that the journey is not a solitary one; the individual, while a singular entity, is an integral thread in the composition of the team. The paradox of teamwork lies in the understanding that while there is no "I" in "team," there is an "I" in "win," symbolizing the individual's role in the collective success.

What I'm getting at here is that leadership is the beacon that guides this endeavor. It's the act of nurturing and forging relationships, fostering the growth of opportunities, and instilling the discipline required for others to achieve their goals. True leadership is defined as selflessness by the elevation of others for their benefit rather than one's own. These are amazing thoughts by an amazing leader. Remember, there is always more to the story.

One thing I forgot to mention: I don't even like Alabama!

Our Responsibility as Leaders

Now, we've followed our journey from the engagement dilemma to the neuroscience of coaching. We've climbed from the basecamp of shared vision and aligned mission to scales the ridgelines of situational conversations with fluency. However, none of this will have an impact if we, as coaches, don't consistently reinforce our coaching with multiple scenarios.

After years of training the NeuroSelling process, we constantly hear sales leaders comment that their account managers need to be pre-planned, prepared, practiced, and performed (more P words). Yet, when it comes to coaching, I ask them how intentionally they prepare their coaching conversations. I usually get a blank stare. The answer is almost always the same: "I'll prepare when HR is involved, or it is a 'tough' conversation." That's fine, but it isn't good enough.

Coaching reinforcement means that we study the art of leadership and coaching. We prepare our conversations through a framework that has impact; if you don't use this one, use something else. Find a coaching accountability partner and grow together. If you need it, hire an outside coach or consulting group to help you. In the art of communication, I fundamentally believe that the moment you choose to suit up and wear the armor of a leader/coach, the impact on your players and performance is in your hands. As you know and we've stated, you can no longer win on your own.

Top NeuroCoaching Takeaways

1. **Coaching is about realizing the full story.**

   Leaders and coaches must recognize that every individual is more than just one moment or chapter in their journey. Judging someone based on a single event or conversation can lead to misunderstandings. True coaching requires understanding a person's full story, their pressures, and their potential.

2. **Intentionality in coaching drives performance.**

   A structured approach to coaching, as shown in the NeuroCoaching framework, ensures consistency in leadership development. Organizations that lack structure will struggle to create a culture of high-performance coaching and communication.

3. **Leadership requires both relational and transactional coaching.**

   Great coaches, like Nick Saban, balance relational coaching (building trust, fostering relationships) with transactional coaching (performance metrics, discipline, structured plans). Effective coaching is about reading the situation and adjusting as needed.

4. **Coaching requires pre-planning, not just for tough conversations.**

   Many leaders only prepare for coaching when HR is involved or when the conversation is difficult. However, high-impact coaching requires regular reinforcement, scenario planning, and accountability. Just like in sales, coaching should be pre-planned, practiced, and continuously refined.

CHAPTER 16

PUTTING IT ALL TOGETHER: CREATING COACHING COMMUNICATION HABITS

We are what we repeatedly do. Excellence, then, is not an act but a habit.

—WILL DURANT

THE MORNING SUN filtered through the blinds, casting stripes of light across my bedroom floor. As I rolled out of bed, my feet found the familiar spot on the carpet, just inches from the slippers I always kept there. I made my way to the bathroom. Then, without even thinking, I wandered into the kitchen, letting the dog out of the same mudroom door as every day before. While waiting for her to return, I reached for the mug from the same spot in the cabinet without a second thought. I poured the coffee, added the same amount of cream, and took that first sip. I put food and water in the dog's dish and took my usual seat at the kitchen table. As the warm liquid filled me with energy, I smiled, realizing this wasn't just routine—it was efficiency. My brain had mastered the art of starting my day without needing to expend extra energy on the mundane details.

How incredible is that?

Sitting at the kitchen table, I read my morning devotional, then I opened my laptop to check my email. As I scrolled through the messages, I noticed how my hand automatically moved the mouse to delete the junk mail. I barely had to glance at the subject lines to know what could be tossed. It was as if my brain had sorted through this task for me, freeing up mental space for more important things.

I've done this so many times, and now it's second nature. This is the brain at its best—creating pathways that make life easier.

As I moved through my workday reflecting on just how many built-in "habits" I had created, I felt a deep appreciation for these unconscious and, ideally, very efficient behaviors. Every keystroke, every click of the mouse was part of a finely tuned system that allowed me to work with ease. I wasn't just going through the motions; I was benefiting from the countless times my brain had reinforced these actions. It struck me that habits weren't something to escape from but something to embrace. They were evidence of my brain's incredible ability to adapt and streamline my life.

Just then, a member of my team popped their head in and asked me a question that triggered an unexpected emotion, causing me to respond in a less-than-productive manner. As he slowly backed out of my office with a slight look of terror on his face, he said, "I see that I interrupted you and this isn't a good time. I'm sorry. I'll check back in later," and then he left. I started to go back to the task I was working on when it hit me square between the eyes. I have "habits" built in nearly every area of my life, designed to make things more efficient and more productive. Most of these habits have been built intentionally through a repeated routine that drives a desired result. As I reflected on the conversation that had just taken place, I realized that the very thing I teach, the very subject I'm a supposed expert on, communication, is merely another area in which we, as humans, rely almost exclusively on habit. Why I had never thought of this before is beyond me, but there I was, sitting face-to-face with the overwhelming feeling that I had never intentionally developed the right communication "habits." How many areas of my life have been negatively impacted by this? My employees, my peers, my wife, my kids—heck, everyone I interacted with on a daily basis was a receiving party to my communication habits!

Creating Communication Habits: The Conscious Competence Model

You can probably see where I am going. The vast majority of us communicate intuitively, not intentionally—and therefore not very consistently. Coaching is a perfect example of how this concept has a direct and measurable impact on you, your team, and your company. By now, we've covered a great deal of ground, giving you an entirely new set of coaching tools in your toolbox. The challenge from here is in the activation and application of these tools. If you casually read this book in the hopes that these concepts will somehow magically show up in your coaching conversations right when you need them, trust me, they won't. Every habit you've created has taken time and repetition to master. From the simplest habits like brushing your teeth to more complex habits like driving, you have refined these behaviors into skills and those skills into unconscious habits through repetition.

In the context of habit formation, the "four stages of competence," or the "conscious competence"[1] learning model, illustrates the psychological journey from being unaware of a skill to mastering it. These stages reflect how habits are built and ingrained in our behavior, requiring different levels of awareness and practice at each step. Individuals may be at different stages for various skills, and maintaining a high level of competence in any habit often requires consistent practice.

The model begins with unconscious incompetence, where individuals are unaware of their lack of ability in a particular skill. As they become conscious of this gap, they enter the conscious incompetence stage, where they recognize their shortcomings and the value of developing the skill. With continued effort, individuals reach conscious competence, where they can perform the skill, though it requires significant focus and intention. Over time, with enough repetition, the skill becomes second nature, leading to unconscious competence, where the skill becomes a habit and is performed effortlessly and automatically.

The four stages:

1. **Unconscious Incompetence**: The individual is unaware of their lack of skill and may not see the value in the habit. Recognizing the gap and the importance of the eventual habit is essential before moving forward.

2. **Conscious Incompetence**: The individual becomes aware of their deficiency and understands the need for the future habit. Mistakes are common and an important part of learning at this stage.

3. **Conscious Competence**: The skill is learned and can be performed, but it requires significant focus and conscious effort. Distractions can cause a lapse in the skill.

4. **Unconscious Competence**: The skill is so well-practiced that it becomes automatic and can be performed with little or no conscious thought. The individual may even teach the habit to others, depending on how it was learned.

Imagine you're a coach in a corporate setting tasked with guiding a sales team through a transformative process. Your role is not only to impart knowledge but also to facilitate real change in behavior—a task that requires mastery of your own coaching skills. As you embark on this journey, you find yourself moving through the very stages of competence you are helping others navigate.

At the outset of your coaching career, you were likely in the *unconscious incompetence* stage. You might have been unaware of the nuances and complexities involved in truly effective coaching. Perhaps you believed that simply sharing knowledge or offering advice was enough. It wasn't until you encountered the challenges of real-world coaching—resistant team members, inconsistent results, and a lack of engagement—that you began to recognize the gaps in your approach. This is when you entered the *conscious incompetence* stage.

In this stage, you became acutely aware of your shortcomings as a coach. You understood that coaching was more than just giving instructions—it required empathy, active listening, and the ability to tailor your approach to each individual's needs. You started to seek out resources, attend workshops, and learn from more experienced coaches. Every coaching session became a learning experience, and mistakes, though frustrating, were opportunities for growth.

With time and dedication, you progressed to the *conscious competence* stage. You developed a structured approach to coaching, carefully planning each session, anticipating potential challenges, and preparing strategies to overcome them. You began to see improvements in your clients' performance, and your confidence grew. However, coaching still required a significant amount of mental effort. You had to remain focused, constantly adjusting your methods and paying close attention to the dynamics within the team.

Eventually, after countless hours of practice and reflection, you reached the stage of *unconscious competence*. Coaching has become second nature to you. You no longer need to think through every step consciously. You intuitively read the room, ask the right questions, and guide conversations in a way that leads to meaningful breakthroughs. You have internalized the principles of effective coaching, allowing you to adapt effortlessly to different situations and individuals. Your ability to coach has become a habit ingrained in your behavior.

Now, here's the good news/bad news part. As you read the previous section, you subconsciously placed yourself in one of those four boxes as a coach. More than likely, you placed yourself in a section higher than your team might place you. Nonetheless, now that you've learned an entirely new approach to coaching with the tools contained in this book, it will naturally require you to go back to the conscious incompetent stage as you begin working through the framework in real time. Depending on your tenure as a coach, you will most likely move into conscious competence very quickly. Then, assuming you have an opportunity to coach on a regular basis, you should have NeuroCoaching as a habit in very short order!

As a coach, your day is filled with various interactions, each presenting a unique opportunity to influence, guide, and support those you're working with. Let's highlight a few scenarios where you might find yourself and explore how understanding the principles of NeuroCoaching can reshape your approach, challenging you to reflect on your current habits.

Scenario 1: The 1:1 Development Conversation

You're scheduled for a 1:1 meeting with a high-potential employee who has been struggling with meeting their targets. In these conversations, your habit might be to jump straight into problem-solving mode, offering advice and strategies you've seen work before. But today, with the principles of NeuroCoaching in mind, you decide to pause. Instead of leading with solutions, you ask questions designed to help them uncover their own insights. You explore their thought processes, listening deeply for underlying beliefs or assumptions that might be holding them back.

Challenge: Reflect on your approach in 1:1s. Do you tend to offer quick fixes, or do you help the individual discover their own solutions? How might shifting to a more inquiry-based approach empower your team members to develop their own critical thinking and problem-solving skills?

Scenario 2: The Pop-Up Conversation

It's the middle of a hectic day, and a team member unexpectedly drops by your office, clearly frustrated with a project. Your habitual response might be to offer immediate reassurance or to downplay the issue, aiming to keep them motivated. However, by applying NeuroCoaching, you recognize the value of addressing the emotion behind their frustration. You take a moment to acknowledge their feelings, creating space for them to express what's really bothering them. You guide the conversation toward identifying the root cause, helping them to see the situation from a new perspective.

Challenge: In pop-up conversations, do you tend to gloss over emotions to get to solutions quickly? Consider how acknowledging and addressing emotions can lead to more productive problem-solving and a deeper level of trust with your team.

Scenario 3: The Observational Skill Follow-Up

After observing one of your team members in a client meeting, you're scheduled to provide feedback. Your usual habit might be to deliver a straightforward critique, pointing out what they did well and where they need improvement. But today, you decide to integrate NeuroCoaching techniques. You start by asking them to self-assess—what did they feel went well, and where did they see room for improvement? This not only encourages self-reflection but also opens the door for a more collaborative discussion about their development.

Challenge: When giving feedback, do you focus more on delivering your perspective, or do you encourage self-assessment and reflection? How could incorporating self-assessment into your feedback sessions lead to greater ownership of growth and development?

Scenario 4: The Team Coaching Session

You're leading a team meeting focused on enhancing collaboration and communication. Historically, you might have approached these sessions with a structured agenda, ensuring every point is covered. But with NeuroCoaching in mind, you choose to open the floor, allowing team members to voice their thoughts and ideas before you lead the discussion. You create a space where the team can explore their dynamics, using open-ended questions to draw out insights and foster a sense of collective responsibility for improvement.

Challenge: In team coaching sessions, do you find yourself sticking rigidly to an agenda, or are you open to allowing the team to steer the conversation? How might giving your team more control over these discussions improve their engagement and ownership of outcomes?

Scenario 5: The Performance Review

You're conducting a performance review with an employee who has had a challenging year. Your typical habit might be to focus heavily on metrics and outcomes, perhaps offering a few suggestions for improvement. However, with NeuroCoaching, you recognize that this conversation is an opportunity to explore the employee's mindset and motivations. You ask them to reflect on their experiences over the year, encouraging them to identify patterns in their performance and consider what changes they might make going forward. This approach not only addresses performance but also supports their long-term growth and resilience.

Challenge: During performance reviews, do you tend to focus mainly on past performance, or do you explore the underlying factors that contribute to it? How could shifting your focus to include mindset and motivation create more meaningful and productive reviews?

These scenarios highlight the variety of situations a coach might encounter and the habitual responses that often accompany them. As you reflect on your own coaching habits, consider how integrating the principles of NeuroCoaching can lead to more intentional, effective interactions. Each of these moments is an opportunity to move beyond automatic responses and create deeper, more impactful connections with those you coach.

This journey highlights a critical insight: Habits, whether in daily routines or professional coaching, are the brain's way of optimizing and simplifying our lives. The more intentional you are in shaping those habits, the more effective and impactful you can become. As you move forward in your coaching conversations, remember that every skill, every piece of knowledge, and every behavior you cultivate can become a powerful habit, leading you and your team toward greater success and efficiency.

Top NeuroCoaching Takeaways

1. **Communication is an intentional habit.**

    Just like daily routines become automatic, our communication patterns—whether productive or unproductive—are shaped by habit. Many people rely on intuition rather than intention when they communicate, which leads to inconsistencies in coaching and leadership. To become an effective coach, leaders must be deliberate in reinforcing strong communication habits through intentional practice.

2. **The four stages of competence apply to coaching mastery.**

    The journey from *unconscious incompetence* (not knowing what we don't know) to unconscious competence (performing a skill effortlessly) requires practice, self-awareness, and repetition. Coaches must recognize that developing effective coaching skills requires moving through these stages intentionally rather than expecting instant mastery.

3. **Coaching conversations should focus on inquiry, not just solutions.**

    Most of us instinctively jump to providing solutions rather than guiding employees toward their own insights. Whether in 1:1 meetings, pop-up conversations, or performance reviews, *shifting from directive feedback to an inquiry-based approach* helps employees develop critical thinking skills, self-reflection, and ownership over their development.

4. **Intentional coaching transforms workplace culture and performance.**

    By integrating NeuroCoaching techniques, leaders can create more meaningful interactions in everyday coaching moments. Recognizing emotional cues, encouraging self-assessment, and fostering psychological safety can lead to more engaged, motivated, and high-performing teams. The key is to move beyond automatic responses and consistently apply intentional coaching strategies.

CHAPTER 17

HOW TO HAVE AN IMPACT AT THE HIGHEST LEVEL

What's your legacy going to be?
—Dan Docherty & Jeff Bloomfield

WE'VE REACHED THE end of our journey! You should now have an effective tool kit that'll help make you a better leader and coach; however, this'll all be for nothing without repetition.

Everything we've discussed, from situational conversations to the neuroscience of coaching, has been about creating sustainable tools that can bolster your communication and, therefore, relationships with your team members. But none of this changes overnight after finishing an excellent book. It takes practice.

Throughout our corporate careers, we believed in this myth that, as managers, we had our own style and approach to coaching. We didn't need a structure to lead . . . right? We realized that this simply wasn't true. For over thirty-plus years of our careers, we weren't given the tools to create sustainable change or growth within the workplace. So instead, we had to create systems that've been scientifically backed and, therefore, shared with you because more than half of the leaders we coach say they struggle communicating. Daily. There's a huge problem in the workforce that we've dissected at length within these chapters. The next step is how you take this information and learn how to use it every day for effective and sustainable change.

It would also be remiss of us to say that reading this book and jotting down a few notes is all you need to turn your company and leadership skills around. No, this is hard work that requires diligence and will be that much harder to keep up in the face of stress. And when you're inevitably overwhelmed with stress, you're not as flexible, not as creative, and not as open to new ideas, and that stress will turn into a cycle that'll only hurt your team's performance further. You must combat it with the tools you're taking away from these chapters.

We used to buy into the belief that leaders need to know everything and, therefore, have all the right answers. But that's not what great leaders actually think. Instead, great leaders try to understand another's perspective and make that understanding a primary, not a secondary, tool when faced with stress. If everyone we coached could look through the lens of someone else's perspective, it would not only downregulate emotion but would also help create a richer, self-discovery, co-generated type of conversation.

Before we leave you, we wanted to share one more example to really drive home the reason behind this book, and that's the windshield versus rearview mirror analogy. Many senior leaders of the Fortune 100 organizations we've worked with have stated they knew when they were off the path. But they didn't know what the plan was and, therefore, couldn't get their team back on track.

Let's think of this moment through the lens of a stoplight. You, as a leader, are driving the company forward, and there are multiple stoplights ahead that you'll need to stop and handle before continuing forward. You can't blow through them. But there are also mirrors and windows in the car to help. There's a windshield that looks ahead and a rearview mirror looking back to where you came from, and both are equally as important. However, you need to concentrate on how much time you spend looking back versus looking ahead, and this requires a higher level of intentionality. Mastering this will allow you to predict outcomes for any given situation and form a framework—or rather, road—that you and your team can drive safely down.

We hope that you now understand that, as leaders, we all have a daily impact on our employees, and this book has tried to make you more self-aware of your coaching styles and the climate you're creating within the office. These questions are meant for you to reflect on what you've learned and how to move forward with positive change that's lasting.

By creating a world-class coaching climate through the foundation of a shared vision, aligned mission, situational conversations, and a coaching climate, you, as a leader/coach, are impacting relationships and performance in everything you do.

Jim Collins, in *Good to Great*, introduces the Stockdale Paradox, rooted in Admiral Stockdale's POW experiences, advocating for unwavering faith amidst adversity while confronting brutal reality. This mindset is pivotal for sustaining a shared vision. In a business context, the Stockdale Paradox suggests that leaders should have the resolve to face difficult situations and the courage to work through them while simultaneously maintaining faith in the eventual success of their ventures.[1] It's about balancing realism and optimism, ensuring that neither unfounded hope nor despair dominates one's approach to challenges. This paradox is often cited as a key principle for resilience and success in leadership, business, and personal endeavors.

Dissemination of information isn't proper communication. There needs to be a shared understanding in order to communicate well, and that can't happen if leaders continue to undervalue communication with their teams. This entire book is about creating a system of coaching that can allow you to live out your purpose and your team's purpose better. It's a playbook—one that breaks down the science of how our brains react and guidelines to actually coach those you've been entrusted to lead.

We've reached the end of our journey. But in many ways, this is where the real work begins.

Throughout this book, we've explored the principles, tools, and neuroscience behind great coaching. We've equipped you with a framework for building meaningful conversations, unlocking potential, and fostering resilience. But the true power of this work is not found in theory—it's found in the real, lived experiences of the thousands of leaders who've chosen to embrace NeuroCoaching.

We've seen exhausted managers become empowering mentors. We've seen disengaged teams reawaken with purpose and unity. We've seen once-siloed departments begin to collaborate with trust and intention. These aren't just leadership wins. These are deeply human moments of growth that ripple far beyond the boardroom.

This book, this process, is more than professional development—it's personal transformation. When you learn to coach with empathy, presence, and science-backed intentionality, you begin to see people differently. You begin to lead with more clarity. You begin to change the trajectory of not just performance but the emotional climate of your team. That is impact. That is legacy.

Yet none of this happens without consistency. Without reps. Without showing up—even on the hard days—with a commitment to be the kind of leader who doesn't just direct traffic but clears the road.

We used to believe that coaching was just a natural trait—that some people just "had it." We hope you have learned that many of us are blessed with intuitive coaching skills, and it takes discipline to build upon intuition to intentionality. Great leaders don't always have the answers. What they *do* have is the courage to ask better questions, the humility to listen, and the ability to create safe spaces for others to grow. They lead from the windshield, not the rearview mirror—anchored in perspective but focused on the road ahead.

So, yes, keep building your coaching skills as if your life depended on it—because the lives and experiences of those you lead will be forever shaped by your willingness to grow. Just like the mountain we've climbed together throughout these chapters, your journey as a leader/coach is a series of elevations: new challenges, deeper purpose, clearer vision.

Before you go, take a moment to answer these coaching questions honestly and intentionally:

1. What's the one coaching habit I commit to improving this month?

2. How will I measure my coaching impact?

3. Who can hold me accountable for staying on track?

This isn't just a book. It's a call to lead differently, and you now carry a proven playbook—one that we hope will serve not only your business outcomes, but the human beings behind them. Because if we can shift the climate of communication, we can shift the culture. And when we shift the culture, we can change everything.

Here's to leading with purpose.

Here's to coaching with impact.

We'll be rooting for you—every step of the way.

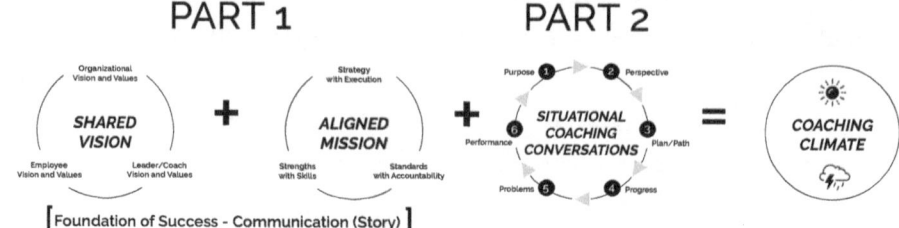

READY TO TAKE THE NEXT STEP WITH NEUROCOACHING?

For more information, visit us at

http://www.braintrustgrowth.com

For program inquiries to have
NeuroCoaching brought to your organization:

support@braintrustgrowth.com

To inquire about having Dan or Jeff
speak at your next event:

dandocherty.com

jeffbloomfield.com

ACKNOWLEDGMENTS

WE'D LIKE TO thank our incredible team at Braintrust. Your dedication to excellence and your passion for this work inspire us every day. We are honored to do this work with you.

To our clients, thank you for trusting us with NeuroCoaching. From our very first client, when we saw NeuroCoaching come to life, we knew this approach to communication and leadership coaching could make a profound impact—both personally and professionally. We are grateful that you continue to trust us, challenge us, and thrive using the principles in this book—your growth is the greatest reward of all.

Dan

First and foremost, I want to thank my wife, Amy. You've always stood by my side and encouraged me to chase my dreams, including earning a PhD—even when most people thought I was crazy. Your unwavering belief in me made all the difference. Forever and always!

To my kids, Abby, Andrew, and Kayla: Your love, support, and the time you sacrificed for me throughout this journey mean more than you'll ever know. Keep chasing your dreams with passion and purpose—I'll always be cheering you on.

To my friend, co-creator, and business partner, Jeff Bloomfield: thank you for your vision, collaboration, thoughtful challenges, and steadfast commitment to NeuroCoaching and this project. It wouldn't be what it is without you.

To my team at Case Western Reserve University—Richard, Ellen, Tony, and Phil—you fundamentally transformed the way I view neuroscience, leadership, and coaching. I'm grateful for your mentorship and insight.

Madison, Melinda, and Beth, thank you for your hard work and support of this project, hours of editing, and for always nudging me forward to write this book. Your encouragement and input mattered.

To our readers, know this: Every conversation is a situational moment of impact. What you do matters deeply to those you lead and serve.

And finally, to my extended family and leaders who have shaped my journey along the way, thank you from the bottom of my heart.

Jeff

I'd like to express my deepest gratitude to my family for their unwavering support and encouragement during the sometimes distracted, long hours through this journey. A special thanks to my co-author, collaborator, and friend, Dan Docherty, PhD, whose brilliance, passion for neuroscience, and commitment to human transformation made this book possible.

BIBLIOGRAPHY

Chapter 1

Baker, Erik. "The Age of the Crisis of Work: What Is the Sound of Quiet Quitting?" *Harper's Magazine*, May 2023. https://harpers.org/archive/2023/05/the-age-of-the-crisis-of-work-quiet-quitting-great-resignation/.

Harter, Jim. "US Employee Engagement Sinks to Ten-Year Low." Gallup, January 14, 2025. https://www.gallup.com/workplace/654911/employee-engagement-sinks-year-low.aspx.

Nolan, Tom. "The Number One Employee Benefit That No One's Talking About," Gallup. https://www.gallup.com/workplace/232955/no-employee-benefit-no-one-talking.aspx.

Chapter 2

Gallup. "Gallup's Employee Engagement Survey: Ask the Right Questions with the Q12 Survey." https://www.gallup.com/q12/.

Gallup. "State of the Global Workplace: 2024 Report," https://www.gallup.com/workplace/349484/state-of-the-global-workplace.aspx.

Goleman, Daniel, Richard E. Boyatzis, and Annie McKee. *Primal Leadership: Unleashing the Power of Emotional Intelligence*. Harvard Business Review Press, 2013.

Greenwood, Kelly, Vivek Bapat, and Mike Maughan, "Research: People Want Their Employers to Talk About Mental Health." *Harvard Business Review*, October 7, 2019, updated November 22, 2109. https://hbr.org/2019/10/research-people-want-their-employers-to-talk-about-mental-health.

Groysberg, Boris, and Michael Slind. "Leadership Is a Conversation." *Harvard Business Review*, June 2012. https://hbr.org/2012/06/leadership-is-a-conversation.

Hernandez, Laura. "The Great Resignation: How to Fight for Talent," Nailted, September 8, 2022. https://nailted.com/blog/the-great-resignation-how-to-fight-the-battle-for-talent/.

Chapter 3

Boyatzis, Richard E. *The Science of Change: Discovering Sustained, Desired Change from Individuals to Organizations and Communities.* New York: Oxford University Press, 2024.

Boyatzis, Richard E., and Anthony I. Jack. "The Neuroscience of Coaching." *Consulting Psychology Journal Practice and Research* 70, no. 1 (2018): 11–27. https://doi.org/10.1037/cpb0000095.

Boyatzis, Richard E., Kylie Rochford, and Scott N. Taylor. "The Role of the Positive Emotional Attractor in Vision and Shared Vision: Toward Effective Leadership, Relationships, and Engagement." *Frontiers in Psychology* 6, Article 670 (2015). https://doi.org/10.3389/fpsyg.2015.00670.

Boyatzis, Richard E., Melvin L. Smith, and Ellen Van Oosten. *Helping People Change: Coaching with Compassion for Lifelong Learning and Growth.* Harvard Business Review Press, 2019.

Boyatzis, Richard E. "Visioning in the Brain: An fMRI Study of Inspirational Coaching and Mentoring," *Social Neuroscience*, 2013.

Kahneman, Daniel. *Thinking, Fast And Slow.* Farrar, Straus and Giroux, 2011.

Chapter 4

Barello, Stephanie Hugie. "Consumer Spending and US Employment from the 2007–2009 Recession Through 2022." US Bureau of Labor Statistics, October 2014. https://www.bls.gov/opub/mlr/2014/

article/consumer-spending-and-us-employment-from-the-recession-through-2022.htm.

Bloomfield, Jeff. *NeuroSelling: Mastering the Customer Conversations Using the Surprising Science of Decision Making.* Axon Publishing, LLC, 2020.

Brown, Brené. *Dare to Lead: Brave Work, Tough Conversations, Whole Hearts.* Penguin Random House, 2018.

Duca, John V. "Subprime Mortgage Crisis 2007–2010: How and Why the Crisis Occurred." Federal Reserve History. https://www.federalreservehistory.org/essays/subprime-mortgage-crisis.

Gruenewald, Tara L., Margaret E. Kemeny, Najib Aziz, and John L. Fahey. "Acute Threat to the Social Self: Shame, Social Self-Esteem, and Cortisol Activity." *Psychosomatic Medicine* 66, no.6 (Nov–Dec 2004): 915–24. https://pubmed.ncbi.nlm.nih.gov/15564358/.

Jack, Anthony I., Richard E. Boyatzis, Masud S. Khawaja, Angela M. Passarelli, and Regina L. Leckie. "Visioning in the Brain: An fMRI Study of Inspirational Coaching and Mentoring." *Social Neuroscience* 8, no. 4 (2013): 369–384. https://doi.org/10.1080/17470919.2013.808259.

MacLean, Paul D. *The Triune Brain in Evolution: Role in Paleocerebral Functions.* Plenum Press, 1990.

Siegel, Dan. "Dr. Dan Siegel's Hand Model of the Brain." August 9, 2017, YouTube, 8:15. https://www.youtube.com/watch?v=f-m2YcdMdFw.

US Department of the Treasury. "Press Release: Statement for the Treasury Borrowing Committee of the Securities Industry and

Financial Markets Association," May 3, 2010. https://home.treasury.gov/news/press-releases/tg683.

Zak, Paul J. "The Neuroscience of Trust: Management Behaviors That Foster Employee Engagement." *Harvard Business Review*, January–February 2017. https://hbr.org/2017/01/the-neuroscience-of-trust.

Chapter 5

Belichick, Bill, Maxx Crosby, Peter King, and Jim Gray, hosts. Let's Go Podcast. Season 4 episode 37, "Week 19: Eric Dickerson and Bill Cowher." NBC Sports, January 6, 2025. https://podcasts.apple.com/us/podcast/lets-go-with-bill-belichick-maxx-crosby-peter-king-jim-gray/id1584409759.

IKEA. "From Humble Origins to a Global Brand: A Brief History of IKEA." https://www.ikea.com/us/en/this-is-ikea/about-us/from-humble-origins-to-global-brand-a-brief-history-of-ikea-pubad29a981/.

Chapter 6

Bailey, Catherine, and Adrian Madden. "What Makes Work Meaningful—Or Meaningless." *MIT Sloan Management Review* 57, no. 4 (2016): 53–61.

Baumeister, Roy F., and Mark R. Leary. "The Need to Belong: Desire for Interpersonal Attachments as a Fundamental Human Motivation." *Psychological Bulletin* 117, no. 3 (1995): 497–529.

Boyatzis, Richard E., Kylie Rochford, and Scott N. Taylor. "The Role of the Positive Emotional Attractor in Vision and Shared Vision: Toward Effective Leadership, Relationships, And Engagement." *Frontiers in Psychology* 6, Article 670 (2015). https://doi.org/10.3389/fpsyg.2015.00670.

Chick-fil-A. "Our Purpose." Accessed March 25, 2025. https://www.chick-fil-a.com/careers/culture.

Kahn, W.A. "Meaningful Connections: Positive Relationships and Attachments at Work." In *Exploring Positive Relationships at Work: Building a Theoretical and Research Foundation*, edited by Jane E. Dutton and Belle Rose Ragins. Lawrence Erlbaum Associates, 2007.

Klein, Danny. "Chick-fil-A Nearing $19 Billion in Sales." *QSR Magazine*, April 6, 2023. https://www.qsrmagazine.com/growth/finance/chick-fil-nearing-19-billion-sales/.

Kouzes, James M., and Barry Z. Posner. *Everyday People, Extraordinary Leadership: How to Make a Difference Regardless of Your Title, Role, or Authority*. Wiley, 2021.

Sinek, Simon. *Find Your Why: A Practical Guide to Discovering Purpose for You and Your Team*. Penguin Random House, 2017.

Ted Lasso, season 1, episode 8, "The Diamond Dogs." Directed by Declan Lowney, written by Jason Sudeikis, Bill Lawrence, Brendan Hunt, Joe Kelly, Leann Bowen. Aired September 18, 2020, on Apple TV+. https://www.imdb.com/title/tt11193418/?ref_=ttfc_ov.

Chapter 7

Flade, Peter, and Gwen Elliot. "Employees Who Use Their Strengths Outperform Those Who Don't." *Gallup*, October 8, 2015. https://www.gallup.com/workplace/236561/employees-strengths-outperform-don.aspx.

Krzyzewski, Mike. *The Gold Standard: Building a World-Class Team*. Grand Central Publishing, 2010.

Krzyzewski, Mike, and Donald T. Phillips. *Leading with the Heart: Coach K's Successful Strategies for Basketball, Business, And Life*. Warner Business Books, 2001.

Chapter 8

Anderson, Robert J., and William A. Adams. *Scaling Leadership: Building Organizational Capacity and Capacity to Create Outcomes that Matter Most*. Wiley, 2019.

Blanchard, Ken. "Three Enduring Truths about Leading Others." Blanchard Leader Chat. https://resources.blanchard.com/blanchard-leaderchat/ken-blanchard-3-enduring-truths-about-leading-others.

Canaday, Sara. "Situational Fluency: Exploring the Secret Sauce of Leadership." *Psychology Today*, July 19, 2023. https://www.psychologytoday.com/us/blog/you-according-to-them/202307/situational-fluency.

Docherty, Dan. "Master the Playbook: Situational Fluency." Braintrust Growth, September 10, 2021. https://braintrustgrowth.com/master-the-playbook-situational-fluency/.

Pat McAfee, host, The Pat McAfee Show, "Monday February 27, 2023." YouTube, 3:16:40. https://www.youtube.com/watch?v=jyhkqVtjImI.

Thier, Jane. "Thanks to AI, Workers Are Struggling with 'FOBO'—Fear of Being Obsolete." *Fortune*, September 12, 2023. https://fortune.com/2023/09/12/workers-fobo-fear-ai-will-replace-jobs/.

Zucker, Rebecca. "Why Highly Efficient Leaders Fail." *Harvard Business Review*, February 12, 2019. https://hbr.org/2019/02/why-highly-efficient-leaders-fail.

Chapter 9

Pitonyak, John, and Rob Desimone. "How to Engage Frontline Managers." Gallup, August 9, 2022, updated January 19, 2024. https://www.gallup.com/workplace/395210/engage-frontline-managers.aspx.

Ted Lasso. Apple TV. https://tv.apple.com/us/show/ted-lasso/umc.cmc.vtoh0mn0xn7t3c643xqonfzy.

United Nations. "What Is Climate Change." Accessed February 21, 2025. https://www.un.org/en/climatechange/what-is-climate-change.

Chapter 10

Boyatzis, Richard E., and Annie McKee. *Resonant Leadership: Renewing Yourself and Connecting with Others through Mindfulness, Hope, and Compassion.* Harvard Business Press, 2005.

Boyatzis, Richard E., and Daniel Goleman. "Emotional and Social Competency Inventory (ESCI)." Korn Ferry. Accessed February 20, 2025. https://www.kornferry.com/capabilities/leadership-professional-development/training-certification/esci-emotional-and-social-competency-inventory.

Boyatzis, Richard E., and Daniel Goleman. *Emotional and Social Competency Inventory Research Guide and Technical Manual.* Korn Ferry, 2017.

Boyatzis, Richard E. "The Behavioral Level of Emotional Intelligence and Its Measurement." *Frontiers in Psychology* 9 (2018): 1438.

Blanchard, "SLII®: Powering Inspired Leaders." Accessed February 20, 2025. https://www.blanchard.com/our-content/programs/slii.

Bradberry, Travis. "Emotional Intelligence – EQ." *Forbes*, January 9, 2014. https://www.forbes.com/sites/travisbradberry/2014/01/09/emotional-intelligence/.

The Decision Lab. "The Leader-Member Exchange Theory." February 20, 2025. From https://thedecisionlab.com/reference-guide/management/the-leader-member-exchange-theory.

Dweck, Carol S. *Mindset: The New Psychology of Success—How We Can Learn to Fulfill Our Potential*. Random House, 2006.

George, Bill, and Peter Sims. *True North: Discover Your Authentic Leadership*. Jossey-Bass, 2007.

Gerhardt, Megan, Josephine Nachemson-Ekwall, and Brandon Fogel. *Gentelligence: The Revolutionary Approach to Leading an Intergenerational Workforce*. Rowman & Littlefield Publishers, 2021.

Gibbs, Nancy. "Emotional Intelligence: The EQ Factor." *Time Magazine*, October 2, 1995. https://time.com/archive/6727963/emotional-intelligence-the-eq-factor/.

Goleman, Daniel. *Emotional Intelligence: Why It Can Matter More than IQ*. Random House, 2006.

Goleman, Daniel, Richard E. Boyatzis, and Annie McKee. *Primal Leadership: Unleashing the Power of Emotional Intelligence*. Harvard Business Review Press, 2013.

Goldberg, Elkhonon. "Train the Gifted." In *HBR Guide to Emotional Intelligence (HBR Guide Series)*. Harvard Business Review Press, 2017.

Grant, Adam. "Why Emotional Intelligence Is Overrated." World Economic Forum, October 3, 2014. https://www.weforum.org/

stories/2014/10/emotional-intelligence-cognitive-ability-sales-performance/.

Harvard Business Review. *HBR Guide to Emotional Intelligence: Build Trust and Influence. Strengthen Relationships. Lead with Resilience*. Harvard Business Review Press, 2017.

Korn Ferry. "Our Story: History Provides Perspective. Future Inspires Opportunity." Accessed February 20, 2025. https://www.kornferry.com/about-us/our-story.

Kotter, John. *Leading Change, With a New Preface by the Author*. Harvard Business Review Press, 2012.

Pontefract, Dan. "Is Emotional Intelligence the Number One Indicator of a Good Leader?" *Forbes*, November 12, 2022. https://www.forbes.com/sites/danpontefract/2022/11/12/is-emotional-intelligence-the-number-one-indicator-of-a-good-leader/.

Whiting, Kate. "These are the Top Ten Job Skills of Tomorrow—and How Long It Takes to Learn Them." World Economic Forum, October 21, 2020. https://www.weforum.org/agenda/2020/10/top-10-work-skills-of-tomorrow-how-long-it-takes-to-learn-them/.

Chapter 11

Covey, Stephen R. *The 7 Habits of Highly Effective People: Powerful Lessons in Personal Change*. Free Press, 1989.

Chapter 12

Baldoni, John. "The Challenger Disaster: A Dramatic Lesson in the Failure to Communicate." *Forbes*, January 28, 2019. https://www.forbes.com/sites/johnbaldoni/2019/01/28/the-challenger-disaster-a-dramatic-lesson-in-the-failure-to-communicate/.

Bloomfield, Jeff, host. The Braintrust "Driving Change" Podcast. "Isaac Lidsky: Eyes Wide Open," Evergreen Podcasts, November 24, 2020. Podcast, 36 min., 42 sec. https://open.spotify.com/episode/2XrI-o4r8SKktM3UTfYInQk.

Clark, Timothy R. *The Four Stages of Psychological Safety: Defining the Path to Inclusion and Innovation.* Berrett-Koehler Publishers, 2020.

Duhigg, Charles. "What Google Learned from Its Quest to Build the Perfect Team." *The New York Times*, February 25, 2016. https://www.nytimes.com/2016/02/28/magazine/what-google-learned-from-its-quest-to-build-the-perfect-team.html#.

Edmondson, Amy C. "Psychological Safety and Learning Behavior in Work Teams." *Administrative Science Quarterly* 44, no. 2 (1999): 350–383. https://doi.org/10.2307/2666999.

Edmondson, Amy C. *The Fearless Organization: Creating Psychological Safety in the Workplace for Learning, Innovation, and Growth.* Wiley, 2018.

Harris, Hugh. "NASA, the Challenger Disaster, and How One Phone Call Could Have Saved the Crew." The Portalist, January 28, 2019. https://theportalist.com/nasa-the-challenger-disaster-and-how-one-phone-call-could-have-saved-the-crew.

Lidsky, Isaac. *Eyes Wide Open: Overcoming Obstacles and Recognizing Opportunities in a World That Can't See Clearly.* Tarcher Perigree, 2017.

Schauer, Katherine. "NASA's TDRS Era Began During Challenger's Maiden Voyage." NASA, April 4. 2013. https://www.nasa.gov/missions/space-shuttle/nasas-tdrs-era-began-during-challengers-maiden-voyage/.

Teitel, Amy Shira. "What Caused the Challenger Disaster?" HISTORY. https://www.history.com/news/how-the-challenger-disaster-changed-nasa.

Uri, John. "Thirty-five Years Ago: Remembering Challenger and Her Crew." NASA, January 28, 2021. https://www.nasa.gov/history/35-years-ago-remembering-challenger-and-her-crew/.

Yeoh, Ben. "Team Work: What Google Found." Then Do Better. https://www.thendobetter.com/investing/2017/7/23/team-work-what-google-found.

Chapter 13

Chapman, Bob, and Raj Sisodia. *Everybody Matters: The Extraordinary Power of Caring for Your People Like Family*. Portfolio, 2015.

Chapter 15

de Haan, Erik. *Relational Coaching: Journey Towards Mastering One-to-One Learning*. Wiley, 2008.

Dodd, Dennis. "Inside Nick Saban's Coaching Rehab: Resurrecting Careers at Alabama, One Sullied Coach at a Time." CBS Sports, June 15, 2021. https://www.cbssports.com/college-football/news/inside-nick-sabans-coaching-rehab-resurrecting-careers-at-alabama-one-sullied-coach-at-a-time/.

Chapter 16

De Phillips, Frank Anthony. *Management of Training Programs*. Irwin, 1960.

Chapter 17

Collins, Jim. *Good to Great: Why Some Companies Make the Leap . . . And Others Don't*. Harper-Collins, 2011.

ENDNOTES

Chapter 1

1. Jim Harter, "US Employee Engagement Sinks to Ten-Year Low," Gallup, January 14, 2025, https://www.gallup.com/workplace/654911/employee-engagement-sinks-year-low.aspx.

2. Tom Nolan, "The Number One Employee Benefit That No One's Talking About," Gallup, https://www.gallup.com/workplace/232955/no-employee-benefit-no-one-talking.aspx.

Chapter 2

1. Erik Baker, "The Age of the Crisis of Work: What Is the Sound of Quiet Quitting?" *Harper's Magazine*, May 2023, https://harpers.org/archive/2023/05/the-age-of-the-crisis-of-work-quiet-quitting-great-resignation/.

2. Laura Hernandez, "The Great Resignation: How to Fight for Talent," *Nailted*, September 8, 2022, https://nailted.com/blog/the-great-resignation-how-to-fight-the-battle-for-talent/.

3. Kelly Greenwood, Vivek Bapat, and Mike Maughan, "Research: People Want Their Employers to Talk About Mental Health," *Harvard Business Review*, October 7, 2019, updated November 22, 2109, https://hbr.org/2019/10/research-people-want-their-employers-to-talk-about-mental-health.

4. "Gallup's Employee Engagement Survey: Ask the Right Questions with the Q12 Survey," Gallup, https://www.gallup.com/q12/.

5. "State of the Global Workplace: 2024 Report," Gallup, https://www.gallup.com/workplace/349484/state-of-the-global-workplace.aspx.

6. Gallup. (2023). State of the Global Workforce Report. Gallup, Inc. https://www.gallup.com

7. Daniel Goleman, Richard E. Boyatzis, and Annie McKee, *Primal Leadership: Unleashing the Power of Emotional Intelligence* (Cambridge, MA: Harvard Business Review Press, 2013), 22.

8. Goleman, *Primal Leadership: Unleashing*, 18.

9. Boris Groysberg and Michael Slind, "Leadership Is a Conversation," *Harvard Business Review*, June 2012, https://hbr.org/2012/06/leadership-is-a-conversation.

Chapter 3

1   Richard E. Boyatzis and Anthony I. Jack, "The Neuroscience of Coaching," *Consulting Psychology Journal Practice and Research* 70, no. 1 (2018): 11–27, https://doi.org/10.1037/cpb0000095.

2   Richard E. Boyatzis, Melvin L. Smith, and Ellen Van Oosten, *Helping People Change: Coaching with Compassion for Lifelong Learning and Growth* (Cambridge, MA: Harvard Business Review Press, 2019), 86.

3   Anthony I. Jack, Richard E. Boyatzis, Masud S. Khawaja, Angela M. Passarelli, and Regina L. Leckie, "Visioning in the Brain: An fMRI Study of Inspirational Coaching and Mentoring," *Social Neuroscience* 8, no. 4 (2013): 369–384, https://doi.org/10.1080/17470919.2013.808259.

4   Boyatzis, Richard E. *The Science of Change: Discovering Sustained, Desired Change from Individuals to Organizations and Communities*. New York: Oxford University Press, 2024.

5   Boyatzis, et al, *Helping People*, 83.

6   Boyatzis, et al, *Helping People*, 70.

7   Boyatzis, et al, *Helping People*, 70.

8   Anthony I. Jack, Richard E. Boyatzis, Masud S. Khawaja, Angela M. Passarelli, and Regina L. Leckie, "Visioning in the Brain: An fMRI Study of Inspirational Coaching and Mentoring," *Social Neuroscience* 8, no. 4 (2013): 369–384. https://doi.org/10.1080/17470919.2013.808259.

9   Richard Boyatzis, "Visioning in the Brain: An fMRI Study of Inspirational Coaching and Mentoring," *Social Neuroscience*, 2013.

10 Richard E. Boyatzis and Anthony I. Jack, "The Neuroscience of Coaching," *Consulting Psychology Journal: Practice and Research* 70, no. 1 (2018): 11–27, https://doi.org/10.1037/cpb0000095.

11 Richard E. Boyatzis, Kylie Rochford, and Scott N. Taylor, "The Role of the Positive Emotional Attractor in Vision and Shared Vision: Toward Effective Leadership, Relationships, and Engagement," *Frontiers in Psychology* 6, Article 670 (2015), https://doi.org/10.3389/fpsyg.2015.00670.

12 Daniel Kahneman, *Thinking, Fast And Slow* (Farrar, Straus and Giroux, 2011), 21.

13 Kahneman, *Thinking*, 21.

14 Kahneman, *Thinking*, 58.

15 Anthony I. Jack, et al, "Visioning," 369–384.

Chapter 4

1 Dr. Dan Siegel, "Dr. Dan Siegel's Hand Model of the Brain," August 9, 2017, YouTube, 8:15, https://www.youtube.com/watch?v=f-m2YcdMdFw.

2 Paul D. MacLean, *The Triune Brain in Evolution: Role in Paleocerebral Functions* (New York: Plenum Press, 1990).

3 Stephanie Hugie Barello, "Consumer Spending and US Employment from the 2007–2009 Recession Through 2022," US Bureau of Labor Statistics, October 2014, https://www.bls.gov/opub/mlr/2014/article/consumer-spending-and-us-employment-from-the-recession-through-2022.htm.

4 US Department of the Treasury, "Press Release: Statement for the Treasury Borrowing Committee of the Securities Industry and Financial Markets Association," May 3, 2010, https://home.treasury.gov/news/press-releases/tg683.

5 John V. Duca, "Subprime Mortgage Crisis 2007–2010: How and Why the Crisis Occurred," Federal Reserve History, https://www.federalreservehistory.org/essays/subprime-mortgage-crisis.

6 Siegel, "Hand Model."

7 Brené Brown, *Dare to Lead: Brave Work, Tough Conversations, Whole Hearts* (London, UK: Penguin Random House, 2018).

8 Brown, *Dare to Lead*, 32.

9 Brown, *Dare to Lead*, 34.

10 Brown, *Dare to Lead*, 20.

11 Brown, *Dare to Lead*, 20.

12 Paul J. Zak, "The Neuroscience of Trust: Management Behaviors That Foster Employee Engagement," *Harvard Business Review*, January–February 2017, https://hbr.org/2017/01/the-neuroscience-of-trust.

13 Zak, "The Neuroscience."

14 Zak, "The Neuroscience," 47–48.

15 Tara L. Gruenewald, Margaret E. Kemeny, Najib Aziz, and John L. Fahey, "Acute Threat to the Social Self: Shame, Social Self-Esteem, and Cortisol Activity,"

Psychosomatic Medicine 66, no.6 (Nov–Dec 2004): 915–24, https://pubmed.ncbi.nlm.nih.gov/15564358/.

16   Jeff Bloomfield, *NeuroSelling: Mastering the Customer Conversations Using the Surprising Science of Decision Making* (Axon Publishing, LLC, 2020), 38.

Chapter 5

1   "From Humble Origins to a Global Brand: A Brief History of IKEA," IKEA, https://www.ikea.com/us/en/this-is-ikea/about-us/from-humble-origins-to-global-brand-a-brief-history-of-ikea-pubad29a981/.

2   Bill Belichick, Maxx Crosby, Peter King, and Jim Gray, hosts, Let's Go Podcast, season 4 episode 37, "Week 19: Eric Dickerson and Bill Cowher," *NBC Sports*, January 6, 2025, https://podcasts.apple.com/us/podcast/lets-go-with-bill-belichick-maxx-crosby-peter-king-jim-gray/id1584409759.

Chapter 6

1   Richard E. Boyatzis, Kylie Rochford, and Scott N. Taylor, "The Role of the Positive Emotional Attractor in Vision and Shared Vision: Toward Effective Leadership, Relationships, And Engagement," *Frontiers in Psychology* 6, Article 670 (2015), https://doi.org/10.3389/fpsyg.2015.00670.

2   W.A. Kahn, "Meaningful Connections: Positive Relationships and Attachments at Work," in *Exploring Positive Relationships at Work: Building a Theoretical and Research Foundation*, ed. Jane E. Dutton and Belle Rose Ragins (Mahwah, NJ: Lawrence Erlbaum Associates, 2007), 189–206.

3   Roy F. Baumeister and Mark R. Leary, "The Need to Belong: Desire for Interpersonal Attachments as a Fundamental Human Motivation," *Psychological Bulletin* 117, no. 3 (1995): 497–529.

4   Catherine Bailey and Adrian Madden, "What Makes Work Meaningful—Or Meaningless," *MIT Sloan Management Review* 57, no. 4 (2016): 53–61.

5   James M. Kouzes and Barry Z. Posner, *Everyday People, Extraordinary Leadership: How to Make a Difference Regardless of Your Title, Role, or Authority* (New Jersey: Wiley, 2021).

6   *Ted Lasso*, season 1, episode 8, "The Diamond Dogs," directed by Declan Lowney, written by Jason Sudeikis, Bill Lawrence, Brendan Hunt, Joe Kelly, Leann Bowen, aired September 18, 2020, on Apple TV+, https://www.imdb.com/title/tt11193418/?ref_=ttfc_ov.

7   "Our Purpose," Chick-fil-A, accessed March 25, 2025, https://www.chick-fil-a.com/careers/culture.

8   Danny Klein, "Chick-fil-A Nearing $19 Billion in Sales," *QSR Magazine*, April 6, 2023, https://www.qsrmagazine.com/growth/finance/chick-fil-nearing-19-billion-sales/.

9   Simon Sinek, *Find Your Why: A Practical Guide to Discovering Purpose for You and Your Team* (New York: Penguin Random House, 2017), 35.

Chapter 7

1   Mike Krzyzewski, *The Gold Standard: Building a World-Class Team* (New York: Grand Central Publishing, 2010), 180.

2   Peter Flade and Gwen Elliot, "Employees Who Use Their Strengths Outperform Those Who Don't," Gallup, October 8, 2015, https://www.gallup.com/workplace/236561/employees-strengths-outperform-don.aspx.

Chapter 8

1   Jane Thier, "Thanks to AI, Workers Are Struggling with 'FOBO'—Fear of Being Obsolete," *Fortune*, September 12, 2023, https://fortune.com/2023/09/12/workers-fobo-fear-ai-will-replace-jobs/.

2   Ken Blanchard, "Three Enduring Truths about Leading Others," Blanchard Leader Chat, https://resources.blanchard.com/blanchard-leaderchat/ken-blanchard-3-enduring-truths-about-leading-others.

3   Rebecca Zucker, "Why Highly Efficient Leaders Fail," *Harvard Business Review*, February 12, 2019, https://hbr.org/2019/02/why-highly-efficient-leaders-fail.

4   Robert J. Anderson and William A. Adams, *Scaling Leadership: Building Organizational Capacity and Capacity to Create Outcomes that Matter Most* (New Jersey: Wiley, 2019).

5   Sara Canaday, "Situational Fluency: Exploring the Secret Sauce of Leadership," *Psychology Today*, July 19, 2023, https://www.psychologytoday.com/us/blog/you-according-to-them/202307/situational-fluency.

6   Dan Docherty, "Master the Playbook: Situational Fluency," *Braintrust Growth*, September 10, 2021, https://braintrustgrowth.com/master-the-playbook-situational-fluency/.

7   Pat McAfee, host, The Pat McAfee Show, "Monday February 27, 2023," YouTube, 3:16:40, https://www.youtube.com/watch?v=jyhkqVtjImI.

Chapter 9

1. John Pitonyak and Rob Desimone, "How to Engage Frontline Managers," Gallup, August 9, 2022, updated January 19, 2024, https://www.gallup.com/workplace/395210/engage-frontline-managers.aspx.

2. "What Is Climate Change," United Nations, accessed February 21, 2025, https://www.un.org/en/climatechange/what-is-climate-change.

3. *Ted Lasso*, Apple TV, https://tv.apple.com/us/show/ted-lasso/umc.cmc.vtoh0mn0xn7t3c643xqonfzy.

Chapter 10

1. "The Leader-Member Exchange Theory," The Decision Lab, February 20, 2025, from https://thedecisionlab.com/reference-guide/management/the-leader-member-exchange-theory.

2. John Kotter, *Leading Change, With a New Preface by the Author* (Boston, MA: Harvard Business Review Press, 2012).

3. "SLII®: Powering Inspired Leaders," Blanchard, accessed February 20, 2025, https://www.blanchard.com/our-content/programs/slii.

4. Megan Gerhardt, Josephine Nachemson-Ekwall, Brandon Fogel, *Gentelligence: The Revolutionary Approach to Leading an Intergenerational Workforce* (Maryland: Rowman & Littlefield Publishers, 2021).

5. "Our Story: History Provides Perspective. Future Inspires Opportunity," Korn Ferry, accessed February 20, 2025, https://www.kornferry.com/about-us/our-story.

6. Richard Boyatzis and Daniel Goleman, *Emotional and Social Competency Inventory Research Guide and Technical Manual* (Korn Ferry, 2017), 27.

7. Goleman, et al, *Primal*, 20

8. Goleman, et al, *Primal*, 21.

9. Bill George and Peter Sims, *True North: Discover Your Authentic Leadership* (San Francisco, CA: Jossey-Bass, 2007).

10. *HBR Guide to Emotional Intelligence: Build Trust and Influence. Strengthen Relationships. Lead with Resilience* (Boston, MA: Harvard Business Review Press, 2017).

11. Richard E. Boyatzis and Daniel Goleman, "Emotional and Social Competency Inventory (ESCI)," Korn Ferry, accessed February 20, 2025, https://www.kornferry.

com/capabilities/leadership-professional-development/training-certification/esci-emotional-and-social-competency-inventory.

12   Daniel Goleman, *Emotional Intelligence: Why It Can Matter More than IQ* (New York: Random House, 2006), xxiii.

13   Kate Whiting, "These are the Top Ten Job Skills of Tomorrow–and How Long It Takes to Learn Them," World Economic Forum, October 21, 2020, https://www.weforum.org/agenda/2020/10/top-10-work-skills-of-tomorrow-how-long-it-takes-to-learn-them/.

14   Adam Grant, "Why Emotional Intelligence Is Overrated," World Economic Forum, October 3, 2014, https://www.weforum.org/stories/2014/10/emotional-intelligence-cognitive-ability-sales-performance/.

15   Richard E. Boyatzis, Annie McKee, *Resonant Leadership: Renewing Yourself and Connecting with Others through Mindfulness, Hope, and Compassion* (Boston, MA: Harvard Business Press, 2005).

16   Daniel Goleman, et al, *Primal*, xvii.

17   Travis Bradberry, "Emotional Intelligence – EQ," *Forbes*, January 9, 2014, https://www.forbes.com/sites/travisbradberry/2014/01/09/emotional-intelligence/.

18   Richard E. Boyatzis, "The Behavioral Level of Emotional Intelligence and Its Measurement," *Frontiers in Psychology* 9 (2018): 1438.

19   Nancy Gibbs, "Emotional Intelligence: The EQ Factor," *Time Magazine*, October 2, 1995, https://time.com/archive/6727963/emotional-intelligence-the-eq-factor/.

20   Dan Pontefract, "Is Emotional Intelligence the Number One Indicator of a Good Leader?" *Forbes*, November 12, 2022, https://www.forbes.com/sites/danpontefract/2022/11/12/is-emotional-intelligence-the-number-one-indicator-of-a-good-leader/.

21   Elkhonon Goldberg, "Train the Gifted," in *HBR Guide to Emotional Intelligence (HBR Guide Series)*, (Boston, MA: Harvard Business Review Press, 2017).

Chapter 11

1   Carol S. Dweck, *Mindset: The New Psychology of Success—How We Can Learn to Fulfill Our Potential* (New York: Random House, 2006).

2   Stephen R. Covey, *The 7 Habits of Highly Effective People: Powerful Lessons in Personal Change* (New York: Free Press, 1989), 239.

Chapter 12

1   John Uri, "Thirty-five Years Ago: Remembering Challenger and Her Crew," NASA, January 28, 2021, https://www.nasa.gov/history/35-years-ago-remembering-challenger-and-her-crew/.

2   Katherine Schauer, "NASA's TDRS Era Began During Challenger's Maiden Voyage," NASA, April 4, 2013, https://www.nasa.gov/missions/space-shuttle/nasas-tdrs-era-began-during-challengers-maiden-voyage/.

3   Amy Shira Teitel, "What Caused the Challenger Disaster?" HISTORY, https://www.history.com/news/how-the-challenger-disaster-changed-nasa.

4   John Baldoni, "The Challenger Disaster: A Dramatic Lesson in the Failure to Communicate," *Forbes*, January 28, 2019, https://www.forbes.com/sites/johnbaldoni/2019/01/28/the-challenger-disaster-a-dramatic-lesson-in-the-failure-to-communicate/.

5   Teitel, "What Caused."

6   Hugh Harris, "NASA, the Challenger Disaster, and How One Phone Call Could Have Saved the Crew," The Portalist, January 28, 2019, https://theportalist.com/nasa-the-challenger-disaster-and-how-one-phone-call-could-have-saved-the-crew.

7   Amy C. Edmondson, "Psychological Safety and Learning Behavior in Work Teams," *Administrative Science Quarterly* 44, no. 2 (1999): 350–383, https://doi.org/10.2307/2666999.

8   Amy C. Edmondson, *The Fearless Organization: Creating Psychological Safety in the Workplace for Learning, Innovation, and Growth* (New Jersey: Wiley, 2018), 1960.

9   Timothy R. Clark, *The Four Stages of Psychological Safety: Defining the Path to Inclusion and Innovation*, (Oakland, CA: Berrett-Koehler Publishers, 2020), 6.

10 Clark, *The Four Stages*, 72.

11 Charles Duhigg, "What Google Learned from Its Quest to Build the Perfect Team," *The New York Times*, February 25, 2016, https://www.nytimes.com/2016/02/28/magazine/what-google-learned-from-its-quest-to-build-the-perfect-team.html#.

12 Ben Yeoh, "Team Work: What Google Found," Then Do Better, https://www.thendobetter.com/investing/2017/7/23/team-work-what-google-found.

13 Isaac Lidsky, *Eyes Wide Open: Overcoming Obstacles and Recognizing Opportunities in a World That Can't See Clearly* (New York: Tarcher Perigree, 2017).

14 Jeff Bloomfield, host, The Braintrust "Driving Change" Podcast, "Isaac Lidsky: Eyes Wide Open," Evergreen Podcasts, November 24, 2020, 36 min., 42 sec., https://open.spotify.com/episode/2XrIo4r8SKktM3UTfYInQk.

Chapter 13

1 Bob Chapman and Raj Sisodia, *Everybody Matters: The Extraordinary Power of Caring for Your People Like Family* (New York: Portfolio, 2015).

Chapter 15

1 Erik de Haan, *Relational Coaching: Journey Towards Mastering One-to-One Learning* (New Jersey: Wiley, 2008).

2 de Haan, *Relational*, 14.

3 de Haan, *Relational*, 19.

4 de Haan, *Relational*, 6.

5 de Haan, *Relational*, 63.

6 Dennis Dodd, "Inside Nick Saban's Coaching Rehab: Resurrecting Careers at Alabama, One Sullied Coach at a Time," CBS Sports, June 15, 2021, https://www.cbssports.com/college-football/news/inside-nick-sabans-coaching-rehab-resurrecting-careers-at-alabama-one-sullied-coach-at-a-time/.

Chapter 16

1 Frank Anthony De Phillips, *Management of Training Programs* (Homewood, IL: R.D. Irwin, 1960), 69.

Chapter 17

1 Jim Collins, *Good to Great: Why Some Companies Make the Leap . . . And Others Don't* (New York: Harper-Collins, 2011).

ABOUT THE AUTHORS

DAN DOCHERTY, PhD, is chief coaching officer and managing partner of the Leadership Development Practice at Braintrust, leadership professor in the MBA program, and assistant director of the Isaac & Oxley Center for Business Leadership at Miami University. With a PhD in Management from Case Western Reserve University, his research centered on the neuroscience of coaching, development, and performance in leader-team member relationships. A former life sciences executive, Dr. Dan has coached thousands of leaders across the globe and co-created the NeuroCoaching® framework to assist leaders in communicating with impact to build stronger relationships and drive performance.

DANDOCHERTY.COM

JEFF BLOOMFIELD is a leading expert in neuroscience-based communication and the founder of Braintrust. As the creator of the NeuroSelling® and co-creator of NeuroCoaching® programs, Jeff's research and techniques empower leaders, coaches, and sales professionals to build trust and inspire action through brain science, behavioral psychology, and storytelling. His mission is to help people communicate with greater clarity, authenticity, and influence—in both business and life.

JEFFBLOOMFIELD.COM

www.braintrustgrowth.com

www.ingramcontent.com/pod-product-compliance
Lightning Source LLC
LaVergne TN
LVHW041957060526
838200LV00018B/376/J